Teacher Leadership and Behaviour Management

Teacher Leadership and Behaviour Management

Edited by
Bill Rogers

P·C·P
Paul Chapman
Publishing

Paul Chapman Publishing
A SAGE Publications Company
6 Bonhill Street
London EC2A 4PU

SAGE Publications Inc
2455 Teller Road
Thousand Oaks, California 91320

SAGE Publictions India Pvt Ltd
32, M-Block Market
Greater Kailash – I
New Delhi 110 048

Library of Congress Control Number: 2002101932

A catalogue record for this book is available from the British
Library

ISBN 0 7619 4019 7
ISBN 0 7619 4020 0 (pbk)

Typeset by PDQ Typesetting, Newcastle-under-Lyme
Printed and bound in Great Britain by Cromwell Press,
Trowbridge, Wiltshire

Contents

'A teacher should have maximal authority and minimal power'
Thomas Szasz

'Never mind the trick. What the hell's the point?'
(p 122 in Joseph Heller's *Catch 22*).

Introduction

Our aim in this book has been to address current trends and approaches in behaviour leadership in terms of practical considerations about behaviour management and discipline in today's schools. The emphasis on teacher leadership is purposeful; we believe that the kind of teacher leadership significantly impacts on the effectiveness and humanity of discipline and management.

Although the term 'current' is utilised, I believe that some aspects of teacher leadership behaviour and practice are unchanging and axiomatic – not dependant on time, place, age, context or culture. I have sought to address these discipline and management practices in the first essay. This essay addresses the issue of 'what changes' and 'what stays the same' with respect to teacher leadership and behaviour as it affects discipline and management in today's schools.

While there have obviously been significant changes in society in the late 20th century, some aspects of humane, constructive, positive discipline do not fundamentally change, even in a so-called 'post-modern society'.[1]

The contributors to this book know schools well; they have a considerable and wide experience in education that they bring to the concerns and challenges of today's classrooms. Their professional 'currency' is widely respected in the areas addressed by the essay topics in particular and the topic of the book in general.

While they are mostly working within universities they all have a teaching background and are all directly involved with schools in research and consultancy. In my own case I also engage in peer-mentoring – working with teachers as a coach/mentor in classrooms.

What my colleagues share in these essays comes from a commitment to supporting their teaching colleagues with practical, action-research focused in areas such as: teacher leadership; effective teaching; colleague support; discipline and behaviour management; and working with students who present with emotional-behavioural disorders.

All these facets of *practical* research are here shared with insight, understanding and awareness of current trends and needs. Their focus is firmly grounded in the 'humanist' tradition – not uncritically but with a teacher's eye for balancing research with *realpolitik*. Each writer in their own way addresses changes to the nature of teacher leadership in areas such as 'discipline', 'punishment', 'power', 'control', 'hierarchy', 'rights and responsibilities', 'challenging behaviours' and 'behaviour' arising from emotional and behavioural disorders.

The aim of all behaviour management and discipline is to enable students to take ownership of their behaviour in a way that respects the rights of others. This aim is a constant challenge for teachers when they discipline and manage; each writer seeks to develop management and discipline practices, approaches and skills to enhance that leadership aim.

Dr John Robertson explores teacher leadership from the perspective of 'boss', 'manager' and 'leader'. He contrasts these management styles and practices in a practical and engaging way. John's essay is enhanced by the many typical classroom scenarios teachers face each day when they have to deal with distracting and disruptive student behaviours.

Dr Chris Kyriacou has written widely on the issue of effective teaching and student management. He clearly and helpfully illustrates the link between discipline and 'good teaching' and how any sense of 'effective discipline' is linked to the building of good relationships between a teacher and a class group.

Christine Richmond explores the nature of language in behaviour management, contrasting the differences and effect of teacher language in teacher management. Christine presents a positive and challenging model for teachers to re-assess their management and teaching language.

Tim O'Brien has an amusing title for an empathetic essay on working with students with emotional and behavioural difficulties. Tim has long experience of working with such students and in this essay he explores the key skills and attributes essential to successful and positive practice.

Lynne Parsons shares current trends in the management of emotional and behavioural difficulties. Lynne has wide experience consulting with schools and in this essay shares practical, 'hands-on' strategies to support teachers who work with students who present with emotional and behavioural difficulties through her work in a learning centre with students 'at risk'.

Dr Lorelei Carpenter has addressed an issue of wide concern in schools today – the most ubiquitous behavioural-disorder ADD/ADHD. Many children in our schools now take medication (such as Ritalin or Dexamphetamine) to address this 'condition'. Lorelei helps us to understand and appreciate this (at times) controversial issue. Her response is both humane and helpful to teachers and enables an understanding from which we can more effectively support such students.

Dr Glenn Finger addresses the interesting connection between student behaviour, information technology, and teacher management. He provides a challenging insight into the integral nature of IT and student motivation and behaviour.

Colleague support is crucial to the overall organisational health of a school and, as importantly, to the coping ability of teachers. In this last essay I have addressed the culture of support in schools and developed a framework to both understand and evaluate colleague support in schools.

I want to thank all my colleagues who have contributed their time, energy, knowledge and experience to these issues and topics of current concern. I trust that their professional reflection will encourage and support your own teaching journey.

Dr Bill Rogers
Adjunct Professor (Education)
Griffith University, Queensland, Australia

ENDNOTES FOR INTRODUCTION

1   This is not the text to debate the meaning(s) of 'post-modernism' and 'post-modernist' as they relate to behaviour management. In fact one of the problems in defining such terms is the wide variability in their usage and application – it is as if it depends on who one listens to at any given moment what 'relative' meanings the term (post-modernist/modernism) can contain. I have let my colleagues address the 'current' situations on their terms.

1

What changes and what stays the same in behaviour management?

Dr Bill Rogers

It sounds trite to say that 'schools change and behaviour management must change with it' – there are certainly many books that have that motif somewhere in their text.

We are experiencing the 'IT revolution'; computers will revolutionise the classroom, we are constantly told. Even if we do use computers widely we still have to BUTIC as I've discussed with many students – 'Boot up the *internal* computer'. The first computer created was *the* 'computer' that conceived *and* designed *and* made the computer. Of course it's one thing to 'boot it up' it's another to STBS (surf the brain space) – individually and collectively. Woe betide us if we ever conceive of education (in schools) as merely a 'log on' to a physical computer and then get the information 'on-line' as if that is all that 'education' (as knowledge) is about. Schools are also communities – *local learning communities*. Children do not merely learn content off a screen, they learn *in relationship* to others: their peers; their teachers and their local community. Computers can tap into a 'world wide graffiti board' as well as a 'world wide web' but students will need teachers (on the ground) to enable the contextualisation of information *and learning*. As Dewey (1897) has said, 'all education proceeds by the participation of the individual in the social consciousness. . .' (p77).[1]

Society has changed significantly since post-war Britain when I was white, skinny, freckled, knobbly-kneed (in 'daggy' shorts and cap) and sometimes scared of some of my teachers who smacked, hit and caned me and sometimes pulled my ear (ouch!). No doubt they thought they were doing 'good discipline'.

Good teachers then – as now – rarely needed to use corporal punishment; they eschewed calculated anxiety or fear as a 'technique'; they avoided public embarrassment and shaming as a 'device'; they made an effort to keep the dignity – at least the respect – of the individual intact. I remember such teachers with gratitude and affection.

Schools – thankfully – are generally happier places these days for teachers *and* students. Class sizes are smaller (they need to be!); heaters generally work; some schools even have air conditioners.

TV was a tiny black and white screen just four decades ago; essays were handwritten (even at university); the teacher was almost always 'revered' and addressed as 'Sir' or 'Miss'. If I 'talked' in class it was very 'serious', if I was late for no good reason it was 'serious', if I answered back it was a major crime. We were – almost universally – biddable. The hierarchies were well established – you 'did as you were told'. There are teachers who still pine for those halcyon days. Although I did have a teacher we called 'the fat Welsh git' (no offence to the Welsh you understand) who pushed me too far. I was talking in class (at high school aged 14½). He walked across to my desk and jabbed his index finger roughly in my shoulder – 'Listen Rogers – were you brought up or dragged up!' Well – no one (even a teacher) was going to insult my progeny. I stood up and, heart thumping, said 'It's none of your bloody business!' and walked out to stunned silence (both teacher and class). As I walked past the last row some of my classmates looked up and engaged an eye-contact that said, 'Thanks for being our Trojan Horse . . .' I walked into town, got a delicious cream bun and tea (to calm my nerves) and got a bus home. He never pulled that stunt again. I think – even in 1961 – he realised he might have pushed it a bit too far.

The worm had turned. I mostly got 'in trouble' or 'had detentions', or 'got the cane' for answering back and I only 'answered back' when I thought the teacher was unjust, petty or pathetically trivial (at least in my adolescent perception). Even in primary school I had the ruler across the knuckles and on one occasion had to wear a 'dunce's hat'.[2] In schools today children still 'talk in class', 'talk out of turn', avoid tasks or refuse tasks and answer back and they certainly still bully their peers.

Whenever a group of students meets with their teachers some aspects of behaviour management and discipline should not change. When you get 25–30 children in a small room, with the widest variation in personality, temperament and ability, there are natural energies at work that can significantly affect group dynamics and productive teaching and learning. Those energies are present in behaviours that are distracting, attention-seeking, disruptive or (at times) seriously disturbing. All teachers, at all times, in all contexts have needed to address the dynamics of teaching and learning *and* management *and* discipline as they interact with group dynamics. In this sense there is 'nothing new under the sun'. While society has changed, some features of children's behaviour – particularly in school settings – have not changed. It is my view, my belief, that the discipline and behaviour management of a school community should be based on core values and practices that do not change (despite social and technological changes and new social mores). A teacher – or a community of teachers – never disciplines in a value vacuum. At some stage teachers need to reflect on the values and aims of behaviour management and discipline whether it is addressing typical behaviours such as 'calling out', 'butting in', task-avoidance, overly loud communication or whether it is issues such as verbal or physical aggression, bullying or substance abuse.

Whenever we 'manage' student behaviour we communicate certain values: Do we keep the fundamental dignity, and even respect, of the individual in mind? (That would mean – one hopes – that we would avoid sarcasm, 'cheap-shots', put-downs of any kind when we discipline.) Do we value, and aim for, behaviour ownership when we discipline? A cursory example here may illustrate. When a child has an *object d'art* that interferes with instructional or on-task learning some teachers will walk over to the student's desk and merely take (or snatch) the cards, the mini skateboard, the toy, the secreted Walkman. Other teachers will seek to give some 'behaviour ownership' back to the student: e.g. 'Paul – you've got a mini skateboard on your table...' (sometimes an 'incidental direction' is itself enough for some students. The teacher 'describes' what the student is doing that is distracting, leaving the 'cognitive shortfall' to the student – the description can act as an *incidental* direction. Younger children would need a *specific* direction or reminder about behaviour or rule.) The teacher may then extend the 'description' to a 'directed choice': 'I want you to put it in your locker tray (or bag) or on my table – thanks.' (I've never had a student yet put a distracting *object* on my desk...as an 'option'.) You can imagine what will probably happen if a teacher over-vigilantly snatches a high school student's secreted Walkman, key ring or mobile phone: 'Hey give my **** Walkman back; give it back, you can't take that!' A small discipline issue now becomes a major issue: 'I will have it now *thank you!*' 'No way – no way known' (the student values his Walkman). 'Right! (says the teacher) out – go on, you get out of my classroom...!'

Of course any 'discipline language' depends on factors such as what the teacher has established with the class group in terms of shared rights and responsibilities, core routines and rules for the fair, smooth running of the classroom; the teacher's characteristic tone and manner when they discipline (as above); how they follow-up with students beyond the more public setting and (most of all) the kind of relationship the teacher has built with the class group and its individuals.

CORE 'PREFERRED' PRACTICES OF DISCIPLINE

The following practices of management and discipline have their philosophical and moral genesis in the values discussed earlier; their 'utility' is not separate from their purpose. Teachers need to ask on what basis do they *character-istically* discipline in terms of what they believe, say, do. A teacher's practice needs to be based in principle as well as pragmatism. In those schools that seek to develop a whole-school approach to behaviour management and discipline, staff critically, and professionally, reflect on and appraise their policy and practice in light of their espoused values. The basis for behaviour management and discipline – in terms of school-wide teacher management and discipline behaviour – are here, discussed in terms of *preferred* practices. The term 'preferred' is not accidental; the things that really matter in education cannot really be mandated as if by *fiat*. In this sense our *preferred* practice is based on what we value.

Professional collaboration, shared professional reflection and practice based in colleague support and on-going professional development need to characterise these practices, particularly those that address the discipline behaviour of teachers. These practices reflect unchanging features of good discipline. The broad evaluative qualifier 'good' is not based in mere utility but in the values and purposes on which such discipline is based.

1 The aims of discipline

All management and discipline practice is a teacher's best efforts (bad day notwithstanding) to enable the individual and the classroom group to:

▶ *take ownership of and accountability for their behaviour*; to enable students to develop self-discipline in relationship to others.

▶ *respect the rights of others* in their classroom group/s, and across the school; the non-negotiable rights, in this sense, are the 'right to feel safe', the 'right to respect and fair treatment' and (obviously) the 'right to learn' (within one's ability, without undue or unfair distraction from others, with teachers who reasonably seek to cater for individual differences and needs).

▶ build workable relationships between teacher and students.

In seeking to support the aim of discipline that enables the conscious respecting of others' rights, teachers often develop whole-class student behaviour agreements that specifically address core rights and responsibilities (Rogers 1997 and 2000). Each grade teacher (at primary level) or tutor teacher (at secondary level) will address such fundamental responsibilities such as respect for person and property expressed in basic civility and manners, such as 'please', 'thanks', first name (rather than 'him, 'her', 'she', 'he'), 'ask before borrowing', 'excuse me', etc.; *teaching* basic educational and social considerations such as 'partner-voice' (Robertson and Rogers, 1998, 2000) and 'co-operative talk' during class learning time, how to fairly gain teacher assistance time during on-task learning, etc. Thoughtful routines and rules enable the smooth running of a busy, complex, learning community like a classroom. Teaching routine, and 'making routine routine' (Rogers, 1995) gives direction, focus and security to learning and social interaction.

2 Student behaviour agreements

The rights noted earlier are meaningful only in terms of their responsibilities. Teachers need to discuss these rights *and* responsibilities with their class groups in the establishment phase of the year (Rogers, 1998, 2000). A student behaviour agreement discussed with the class group forms a basis for *any* behaviour management generally – and discipline in particular – as it outlines rights and responsibilities, rules and consequences and a commitment to support students in their learning and responsible behaviour.

Such a student behaviour agreement is published within the first three weeks of the school year and a copy sent home to parent(s) with a supporting letter from the headteacher. Each class thus communicates the whole-school emphasis on behaviour, learning and positive discipline in a document that is *classroom-based* and classroom-focused, in terms of language, understanding and development. A photo of the grade class – with their teacher – can give a positive contextual framework between home and school (see Rogers, 1997 and 2000).

3 The practice of discipline

When engaged in any management and discipline teachers will – wherever possible – avoid any unnecessary confrontation with students. This preferred practice will exclude any intentional, easy, use of put-downs, 'cheap-shots', public shaming, embarrassment or sarcasm (tempting as it might be at times!). Humour (the *bon-mot*, repartee, irony, even farce) will often defuse tension, ease anxiety and reframe stressful reality. Sarcasm, and malicious humour is the pathetically easy power-trip of some teachers and is always counter-productive to co-operative discipline.

A student comes late to class and a teacher asks him why he is late. Apart from the unnecessary and unhelpful interrogative ('why?'), if the teacher's tone is overly, or unnecessarily, confrontational it can lead to adverse outcomes.

It is the second occasion in this high school class that the student has arrived late. The teacher is engaged in whole-class teaching:

T: 'Why are you late?!' (It often doesn't matter – at this point in a lesson – *why* the student is late.)
S: (A little 'cocky'; his body language is a little insouciant.) 'People are late sometimes you know . . . gees!'
T: (The teacher doesn't like his attitude, he senses a 'need to win' here.) 'Don't you talk to me like that. Who do you think you are talking to?!'
S: 'Well you don't have to hassle me, do you?'
T: 'I'm not hassling you! I asked you a civil question – I'm not arguing with you . . . right, go and sit over there.' (He points to the two spare seats left.)
S: 'I don't want to sit there. I sit with Bilal and Troy down the back.'
T: 'Listen; I don't care who you sit with. Did I ask you who you wanted to sit with? If you had been here when you're supposed to you could have sat there but you can't – sit over there.'
S: (The student folds his arms.) 'No way – I'm not sitting with Daniel and Travis – I told you I sit with . .'
T: (The teacher is angry now.) 'Right get out! Go on, get out. If you're late to my

class and you can't do as you're told you can get out! – and you'll be on detention!!'

S: 'Yeah well I'm going anyway – this is a sh*t class. I don't give a stuff about your detention!' (The student slams out of class muttering *en route*.)

It can happen that quickly, that easily. Unfortunately this is not a manufactured example. This is not a 'bad' teacher – as such – but it is an example of unnecessary confrontation.

Same 'discipline' – different teacher, different practice. Student arrives late during instructional time.

T: 'Welcome Jarrod. I notice you're late.' (Her tone is confident, even pleasant.)
S: 'Yeah I was just hurrying and that.' (At this point it doesn't matter if Jarrod is being 'creative' with the truth.)
T: 'I'll have a chat later. There's a spare seat over there.' (Incidental language – she doesn't *tell* him – she describes the 'obvious reality' as it were. Her tone conveys expectation as she turns away from him, giving him 'take-up-time'. She is about to resume whole-class attention – *thus getting the focus back to the teaching and learning* – but he isn't quite finished.)
S: 'I don't want to sit there. I sit with Bilal and Troy.'
T: 'I'm sure you do – those seats down the back are taken. (More, brief, 'description of reality'. The teacher *tactically* ignores the student frown, the low level sibilant sigh, partially agrees with Jarrod and refocuses briefly to the main issue.) 'For the time being there is a spare seat over there. Thanks.' (She adds a future 'choice' as she reads his body language.[3]) 'We can organise a seat change later in the lesson. Thanks.' (She turns away from Jarrod, to convey expectation, confidence and 'take-up-time' [Rogers, 1998]. As she re-engages the class group Jarrod walks off with mild attentional gait which the teacher [wisely] *tactically* ignores at this point [Rogers, 1998].

This 'management transaction' took less time than the example noted earlier. Even in this deceptively fundamental practice of avoiding unnecessary confrontation there is a significant aspect of conscious *skill* in language, tone and manner. It is one thing to state a *preferred* practice in discipline; it is quite another for that practice to be normatively realised in day-to-day teaching. The skills inherent in these 'practices' require conscious reading of management transactions and dynamics in a group context. And in all discipline contexts there is that balance of 'relaxed vigilance' with professional flexibility.

There are occasions when it is appropriate, necessary, to confront a student about their behaviour; *assertively* in tone, manner and language. If a student abusively puts another student down in class, or swears *at* a student or teacher, or engages in sexually harassing communication it is essential the teacher uses appropriate assertive language as a key feature of their discipline – hopefully with confidence and skill. Because the need, and expression, for such teacher behaviour is not normative such assertion can be quite significant in its use.

4 Focusing on primary behaviour

Wherever possible, and wherever appropriate, the teacher will keep the focus of management and discipline on the 'primary behaviour' or issue. Some students are past masters at engaging teachers in 'secondary behaviours' (Rogers, 1997, 1998): the pout, the attentional gait, the skewed eye-contact, the overly ebullient sigh, the time-wasting 'filibuster' ('Other teachers don't care if we chew gum' or 'wear our hats in class' or 'play down-ball in the infant area' or 'ride our bikes across the playground' or 'dance on the tables').

When teachers consciously keep the discipline focus on the 'primary' behaviour or issue, they avoid getting drawn in by the 'secondary' sighs and pouts and re-engage the student on the issue that is relevant and important *now*.

A student secretes his Walkman in his bag (or pocket) during on-task learning time. Instead of taking it off the student and confiscating it the teacher acknowledges its presence and uses a direct (imperative) question (avoid asking *why* – it is often not important, or relevant, why he has a Walkman); imperative questions raise some 'cognitive shortfall' in the student and direct them to *their* responsibility (Rogers, 1998, 2000).

T: 'Paul what's the school rule for Walkmans?'
S: 'Gees – other teachers don't mind if we have them long as we get our work done and that.'

The teacher *tactically* ignores the insipient whine and doesn't get drawn on the relative merits of other teachers' 'justice' ('I don't care what other teachers do . .' or the pointless discursive: '*which* other teachers let you have Walkmans on in class?') Instead she refocuses:

T: 'Even if other teachers do (brief partial agreement) what's the school rule for Walkmans?' (The teacher puts the focus back onto the main – the primary – issue.)
S: (Moaning) 'It's not fair'.
T: (The teacher begins to turn away) 'It may not seem fair to you Paul, it is the school rule. You know what to do.' (She walks away leaving him with a task reminder.) 'I'll come back later to see how your work is going – thanks.'

By giving the student 'take-up-time' the teacher conveys confidence and trust in the student's common sense and co-operation. If he chooses not to put the Walkman away the teacher can give a *deferred* consequence expressed as a 'choice': 'If you choose not to put it away (the teacher is not drawn by his protestations) Paul I'll have to ask you to stay back for "time-in".' This is the known 'follow-up' where the teacher follows up the incident and discusses behaviour with the student.

This discipline approach puts the responsibility back on to the student –

without arguing, without unnecessary drama. The key, of course, is the *certainty* of the consequences if they choose not to co-operate (see later). The 'tribal tom-toms' will soon convey the justice of this approach! No 'choice' in such a context is a 'free choice', it occurs within the framework of the published student-behaviour agreement and – of course – the fair rules and routines established by the teacher with the class group.

It will be important for the teacher to follow up some aspects (or 'displays') of 'secondary behaviours' beyond the classroom context, either in an 'after-class chat' or an interview. Away from the 'audience' of their classroom peers a student is often amenable to a discussion about their 'secondary' as well as their 'primary' behaviour.

5 Least intrusive intervention

Use a least-to-more intrusive intervention approach to management and discipline where possible and where appropriate. The few examples noted thus far illustrate how teachers can often address discipline incidents in a 'least intrusive' way both in discipline language and manner.

THE LANGUAGE OF DISCIPLINE

This is not the text to give extended examples of teacher language and behaviour redolent of positive, co-operative, discipline (see Rogers, 1997, 1998 and 2000; Robertson, 1998; O'Brien, 1999 and Richmond – later in this text). It will be important for teachers to reflect on, and discuss with their colleagues, the nature and purpose of the *language of discipline* with special reference to common values and aims. In many schools colleagues share features of common practice (in discipline) that embrace common aims while allowing professional discretion *within* those aims noted earlier.

RELAXED VIGILANCE

When teachers are engaged in out-of-class duty-of-care (e.g. corridor super-vision, playground supervision, 'wet-day' and 'bus duty') it is important for teachers to be 'relaxedly vigilant' regarding thoughtless, inappropriate, disruptive or hostile student behaviours (Rogers, 2000). Even here the aims and practices of respectful discipline can be realised.

When students are running in the corridor there are many ways in which teachers can be 'least-intrusive' in their discipline.

Teacher (A) calls the students over. They reluctantly come, she *tactically* ignores their demeanour, their low-level whining (the 'secondary behaviour'). She smiles and says, in a quiet confident voice, 'Walking is safer, thank you.'

They return a wry grin and walk off.

Teacher (B) calls the students over and gives a rule reminder, 'Fellas, remember our rule for inside movement. Thanks.'

Teacher (C) calls the students over 'It's David, Chris and Ibrahim. Yes? Boys; can three into one go?' 'Eh?' Chris isn't sure what the teacher is referring to. 'One single door of the double doors is open. Can three into one go?' One of the lads says 'Is this a trick question?' The teacher is about to add 'No it's a fair dinkum question' when Ibrahim grins 'Nope.' 'Sounds like you know what to do – enjoy your playtime.'

In each of these examples each teacher is disciplining in a 'least intrusive' way in language, tone and manner. Each teacher shares the same 'preferred practice'. Each teacher is also 'relaxedly vigilant' about appropriate behaviour. In a 'least-to-most hierarchy' for discipline language, teachers will normally have a wide 'least intrusive' discipline repertoire that includes: non-verbal cueing; incidental language (e.g. 'Lisa and Chantelle, you're talking – I'm teaching. Thank you.' – this to two girls talking while the teacher is engaged in instructional time); behavioural directions that focus on expected behaviour ('Looking this way and listening – now, thank you.') rather than just negatively directing the unacceptable or wrong behaviour (e.g. *'Don't talk* while I'm teaching'; rule reminders e.g. 'Remember our class rule for asking questions.' – this to a group or to named individuals. 'Remember our partner-voice rule thanks' – this to a group or to named individuals.); directed choices (e.g. 'Yes you can go to the toilet when I'm finished reading the story.' – this to a student whose request to go to the toilet seems frivolous.) 'When – then' choices are preferable to overused 'No you can't because . . .' statements. Deferred consequences are also expressed as directed choices (see example noted earlier).

Inherent in any of these practices are significant skills of language, manner and approach in discipline settings – particularly with challenging students who present with emotional and behavioural disorders.

RELATIONAL POWER

Many of the teachers in my childhood used adult power to control children – we got used to the most common, and 'normal', expressions of such power (caning, the strap, the thrown chalk or chalk-duster, lines and more lines . . .). It was an 'occupational' hazard; we lived with it and we had a parental culture that by and large endorsed it.

When teachers use their adult power to discipline children, it is important to reflect on what power(s) they actually have. While we have a certain 'power' within our role, that power is relative to the acceptance given by our students. We also have psychological power that is 'read' by our students in terms of the teacher's ability to confidently lead as an adult *within the role* of teacher. Such psychological power is more to do with relational dynamics, emotional intelligence[3] and the ability to teach than role status.

If we use our 'power' merely to control others; by force, fear, reward or punishment, we convey a particular message – and particular values – about the nature of behaviour and responsibility. Some teachers, even today, seek to use their power to control student behaviour only to get frustrated or angry when students often challenge such power or even resist it. It is easy to 'train' students into believing it is our 'job' to control them, only to end up in a kind of ritual about who has the most power.

There are many children in our school today who will – through behaviour or language – indicate to teachers that 'you can't make me do anything!' They are right – of course – in their own private logic. In no way am I saying I approve of such an attitude, I am merely stating obvious reality. If we are going to work with students in any meaningful and positive way, we need to avoid discipline approaches that easily resort to mere controlling power. This is not easy; it takes some thought, some skill and some shared collegial practice.

It takes some change of pedagogical and psychological mindset to see our power as a teacher as power *for*, and power *with* our students rather than merely power *over* others. In this sense we are using our power (and experience and knowledge – particularly 'emotional intelligence') to work *with* the 'emerging adult' in the child or young person. This is a more difficult, and demanding, conception of adult power to come to terms with. It is not the same as simple control over others. It took me a while as a beginning teacher to work through these differences in understanding and use of power.

We are the adult, we are the teacher leader (imperfect – of course, fallible – yet, adult – none the less). While we should never condone or accede to rude, insouciant, arrogant and defiant behaviour in children we can still use our adult power to reshape the discipline transactions so that we enable the student to 'own' what is happening with his behaviour rather that letting him force us into a power-exchange that gives a student a stage on which he appears to make us control him and then prove we cannot.

In a year 10 class several years ago (my first session with that class) I was coming to the close of a social studies lesson when a female student walked from the back row to the classroom door. She stopped at the door, dropped her bag with a flourish, and stood hand on hip. I was summarising what we had covered as a class group and about to say good-bye (for now) to the class. The bell would go in a few minutes. Her peers, naturally, eyeballed her – she was 'on stage'. I felt the ambient tension (nothing new) and I was aware the other students expected me to 'do something'.

I turned to face her (still standing – front centre – several metres away). 'Rachel, you're out of your seat and the bell hasn't gone yet.' (A description of *obvious* reality – I was hoping for some 'cognitive shortfall' on her part). She looked at me and said (in a sighing, wearied, truculent voice) 'Well if the bell's about to go I might as well stay here.' Her smirk, her shoulder twist, her raised eyes all conveying that this was the start of a 'game'. (I have had colleagues describe such students as having 'slappable faces', a temptation I am *very* familiar with.) I gave her a 'choice' – with a deferred consequence. 'The lesson hasn't finished yet. In our class we leave from our seats when the bell goes. If you continue to stand there, and not leave from your seat, I'll have to follow it up with you after class.' She retorted quickly, (with a well-practised toss of her head) 'I don't care.' I added (as calmly as I could) 'But I care' and redirected my attention back to the class group.

It would be tempting to get drawn into a power struggle, would it not? 'You will care!! Who do you think you're talking to?! I'm 50 years of age (I was then) and I have been teaching for 197 years and no student will talk to me like that!! You're on detention and I'll ring your parents and I'll . . .'

Being calm, even quietly assertive, in such exchanges does not mean we do not convey a confident firmness in what we do and say. Other students (as in this case) take their 'reading' of the situation from their teacher-leader. Here is an example where we are using our power to 'define', to lead, to shape the discipline/management context so that the responsibility 'ball' is back in the right court – with the student.

Using our power to control the *situation* and shape the discipline language, the context and the 'choices' is never easy. Rachel actually looked a little deflated as I took my eyes off her and re-addressed the class for the remaining few minutes before the bell for morning recess. Fortunately they were 'with me'. I strongly suspect, though, that if I had started shouting and gesticulating at her, and threatening her, many of the class group would have sided with Rachel (such is the nature of group dynamics in schools these days).

RUDENESS

If a student's tone of voice is particularly rude, or 'cocky', a firm, brief, assertive 'I' statement and a redirection to the class rule (or right or expected behaviour) is preferable to contestable, counter-challenging language (even if such is tempting: 'I'll show you. . . !' 'How dare you!' 'I am the teacher and no one speaks to me like that!' – they did).

An 'I' statement needs to look and sound confident and assertive (avoid the jabbing-in-the-air finger). 'I'm not speaking to you rudely' or 'I don't expect you to speak to me rudely . . .'. The teacher should direct or refer to the rule/right and give take-up time where appropriate. If the student continues being rude, challenging or threatening the teacher should utilise time-out options immediately. In such cases time-out options must have school-wide colleague support and back-up. In the short term it often involves the teacher not giving unnecessary 'wind' to the student's power-seeking 'sails' (easier said than done) and making a serious effort to follow-up with them away from their audience of peers. Such follow up involves helping the student to be fully aware of how they are using their power and how they can redefine such power productively. This is the approach I took with Rachel – we even got to tolerate each other with basic civility in the days following this incident.

MORE/MOST INTRUSIVE

There are occasions when it is entirely appropriate – indeed essential – for a teacher to communicate appropriate (and necessary) anger. On such occasions it is still possible to discipline in ways that keep the basic dignity and respect of the individual (or group) intact.

▶ Get angry on issues that matter. Anger is different in *degree* from common annoyance, irritation, or frustration. One would hope that teachers need not get *angry* about uniform misdemeanours, uncompleted homework, students without equipment, 'chatty' students etc. If we overuse the *word* anger (as well as the assertive expression of our anger) we devalue the moral currency – and weight – of anger.

▶ Be aware of situations, behaviours and even individuals that lower your tolerance levels – particularly the typical 'secondary behaviours' noted earlier.

▶ Calm yourself (briefly, consciously) before seeking to 'calm' the other person. This very difficult principle is crucial when working with irrationally angry parents!

▶ When communicating one's anger *to* the other person (particularly children):
  – keep the anger message brief
  – focus (and keep the focus) on the issue or behaviour you are angry about rather than attacking the person (tempting as it may be)
  – de-escalate the natural arousal after having assertively communicated your anger. Children are often not naturally practiced at de-escalating feelings of arousal and conflictual tension
  – allow some necessary cool-off-time (or directed 'time-out') following anger communication
  – always 'repair and rebuild' after cool-off-time with group or individual. Repairing and rebuilding gives the opportunity for both student and teacher to learn and grow from anger-arousing episodes. It is worth recalling the apostle Paul's advice 'not to let the sun go down on your anger' (Ephesians Chapter 4. New Testament).

▶ Follow up and follow through on issues that matter. Some behaviours need follow-up even if the teacher has already exercised some correction or discipline in the short term. Follow-up emphasises to students (and parents) that some issues, some behaviours, need addressing beyond the more public sphere (of classroom or playground) – away from the audience of a student's peers. In this longer-term context a teacher can clarify their concerns about a student's behaviour (and learning) as well as inviting understanding and co-operation and offering support.

▶ When applying behaviour consequences (or punishment) emphasise the certainty of the consequence rather than the severity of the consequence. Some teachers will keep a student back after class (or during detention) and add to any fair 'certainty' unnecessary 'emotional pay-back' 'You could be outside playing with your friends now, couldn't you? But you're not, you're in here! You said before that you didn't care – you're caring now, aren't you?!'

▶ When applying consequences, a preferred practice could well include the 3Rs principle: keep the consequences as *related* as possible (so the student – hopefully – may learn something from the consequence); keep the consequence *reasonable* (a degree of seriousness relative to the disruptive or wrong behaviour) and – the most difficult (at times) – keep the *respect* intact. Some consequences in schools need to be non-negotiable (harassment, bullying, substance abuse, aggression, violence, weapons); many consequences, however, will be 'negotiable'. One of the most commonly used unrelated consequences I had as a student was 'lines'. If we are going to use writing as part of the consequential due process at least we can seek to make it relate to the behaviour that the child is in detention for. For many years now I've found it helpful to use a written proforma (two-sided A4) with the following questions: *What happened? What is your side of the story? What rule/right was affected by your behaviour? What can you do to fix things up?* (or *make things better?* or *work things out?*) An ancillary question is also appropriate: *How can I help to...?* It is not how much a student writes but what he writes – teachers can use the writing as part of the 'repairing and rebuilding' process.

If a student is engaged in repeated – similar – behaviour it will be more effective to develop an individual behaviour management plan based in on-going case-supervision by a teacher skilled in behaviour therapy and special needs. (See Rogers 1994 and 2000.)

TIME-OUT

A key behavioural consequence in school discipline policy – and practice – is the use of 'time-out' when students are behaving in repeatedly disruptive ways in the classroom (or playground), or are being hostile or aggressive. 'Time-out' policy needs to include both in-class options and exit-from-class options. No teacher should have to suffer the indignity of any student effectively holding the classroom, or playground, 'to ransom'. Policy on time-out should be clearly explained to parents and students and the practice of any time-out should be practical and achievable.

All time-out should be followed up by the initiating teacher to work through any further consequences and (of course) to 'repair and rebuild'. If a student has been in time-out several times (in close succession) it will be imperative for senior staff to support grade/subject teachers by developing an individual behaviour management plan for the student in question (Rogers, 1994, and 2000).

WHOLE-SCHOOL POLICIES

Utilise wide colleague support in planning discipline policy; developing whole-class student behaviour agreements; developing school-wide preferred practices for management and discipline; developing classroom and playground plans for behaviour management/discipline (Rogers, 1995); developing time-out options, particularly colleague-assisted time-out (Rogers, 1998 and 2000); developing individual behaviour management plans and continuing needs-based opportunities for professional development and most of all opportunities for off-loading concerns about discipline without censure (Rogers, 2001).

Being thoughtfully reflective about our discipline practice is an important first step in considering not only what we do in management and discipline but what we *should* do. The reasons for disruptive behaviour in schools are complex at times; there are many reasons why a student is attentional, distracting or disruptive. Those reasons are clearly affected by 'causative pathologies': dysfunctional family behaviour; structural poverty; long-term parental unemployment; absentee fatherhood; parental substance abuse; emotional, physical and psychological abuse. Their disruptive behaviour may also be affected by a 'need to belong' resulting in significant compensatory behaviours such as frequent attention-seeking and power-seeking. (Dreikurs *et al*, 1982.)

Although disruptive and dysfunctional behaviour is 'conditioned' – or at least significantly affected – by 'causative pathology' (how could it not be?) it is also *learned in context*. Effective and supportive teachers (and schools) do not re-victimise the child at school by saying he/she cannot change patterns of attentional, disruptive or dysfunctional behaviour. (Rogers, 2000). Children spend a third of the waking day at school; for a small percentage of children school can offer a safe, sane, secure place and for *all* children a place to learn about behaviour, about choices and about other pathways in their pre-adult life. Supportive teachers and supportive schools teach behaviour and support behaviour in the context of the school community.

CONCLUSION

Some teachers want guarantees in management and discipline such that if one does 'a', 'b' or 'c' then 'd' and 'e' ought to follow. There is no formula and no guarantees, when it comes to effective discipline. Indeed, even the term 'effective' needs to be considered beyond any mere utilitarian reading ('if it works do it', 'if it shuts them up and gains compliance does it matter what we do?')

No discipline practice is value free. Those preferred practices I have shared here are 'preferred' because of the inherent values they contain, and the purposes to which they are addressed and confirmed in the experience of their use with my colleagues in supportive schools (Rogers, 1995 and 2001). No one preferred practice can be taken by itself; they are all part of the creative tension of our daily work. Taken together they increase the probability of co-operative student behaviour. It is my belief that these preferred practices contain those features of discipline practice that should not change.

Caveat

In the day-to-day *real-politik* of teaching, management and discipline we have our bad days. We may 'snap' at our students, 'mistarget' or 'miscue' – it happens particularly when we're tired, stressed, doing too much on too many fronts. It is important to recognise and acknowledge fallibility in ourselves and others. This does not mean we acquiesce to our fallibility it means that we do not unnecessarily blame or criticise ourselves or others (Rogers, 2001). At times we will need to apologise to our students, and we should always make the genuine effort to repair and rebuild with our students (and colleagues). This will often – more than anything else – give that humanity to our profession that mere technique or skill can never replace.

ENDNOTES

1 'The most formal and technical education in the world cannot safely depart from this general process. It can only organise it; or differentiate it in some particular direction. I believe that the only true education comes through the stimulation of the child's powers by the demands of the social situations in which he finds himself. Through these demands he is stimulated to act as a member of a unity, to emerge from his original narrowness of action and feeling and to conceive of himself from the standpoint of the welfare of the group to which he belongs.' (Dewey, 1897, p77) In Nash, P. (1968) *Models of Men: Explorations in the Western Education Tradition*. New York: John Wiley and Sons.

2 The word 'dunce' is a word introduced by the disciples of St Thomas Acquinas (in the 13th century) to ridicule those who followed the theologian John *Duns* Scotus. It has come to mean someone who is slow-witted, a dullard; in other words, stupid.

3 While a reasonable IQ is helpful as a teacher(!), EQ (emotional intelligence) is probably much more important. EQ involves behaviours such as self and other awareness, impulse control, the awareness of others in terms of 'social deftness' – the ability to 'read' non-verbal cues and interpersonal dynamics and respond adequately. (See Goleman, 1996 and Johnson, 1972.)

REFERENCES

Dewey, J. My Pedagogic Creed *The School Journal* Vol 55. No. 3 Jan 16, 1897, pp 77–80 in Nash, P. (1968) *Models of Men: Explorations in the Western Educational Traditions.* New York: John Wiley and Sons.

Dreikurs, R., Grunwald, B. and Pepper, F. (1992) *Maintaining Sanity in the Classroom* (2nd edn.) New York: Harper and Rowe.

Goleman, D. (1996) *Emotional Intelligence.* London: Bloomsbury.

Johnson, D. W. (1972) *Reaching Out: Interpersonal Effectiveness and Self-Actualisation* (5th edn.) Boston: Allyn and Bacon.

O'Brien, T. (1999) *Promoting Positive Behaviour.* London: David Fulton.

Robertson, J. (1996) *Effective Classroom Control: Understanding teacher-pupil relationships* (3rd edn.) London: Hodder and Stoughton.

Rogers, B. (1994) *Behaviour Recovery:* A whole-school programme for mainstream schools. Camberwell: ACER.

Rogers, B. (1995) *Behaviour Management: A Whole School Approach.* London: Paul Chapman. (In Australia published by Scholastic Books, Sydney.)

Rogers, B. (1997) *Cracking the Hard Class: Strategies For Managing the Harder Than Average Class.* London: Paul Chapman.

Rogers, B. (1998) *You Know the Fair Rule and More.* London: Pitman. (In Australia published by Australian Council for Educational Research – Camberwell, Victoria, Australia.)

Rogers, B. (2000) *Classroom Behaviour: A Practical Guide to Effective Teaching, Behaviour Management and Colleague Support.* London: Books Education.

Rogers, B. (2001) *I Get By With a Little Help...Colleague Support in Schools. (How colleague support can affect individual coping, stress, behaviour management, professional development and change in schools).* Melbourne: Australian Council for Educational Research.

2

The Boss, the Manager and the Leader: approaches to dealing with disruption

One teacher in his time plays many parts.

John Robertson

In any school, on any day, in every classroom there will be a range of management and discipline 'approaches' present. John Robertson explores the salient features, characteristics and behaviours of three 'styles' of management that will immediately resonate with a teacher's experience. He outlines and illustrates (with practical examples) the relative merits, shortcomings and effects of these three 'approaches'.

A key feature of John's contribution is the study he makes of the nature of teacher authority and relational power present in one's management and discipline (a theme explored in several essays in this text).

John goes on to explore the effect of teacher language and non-verbal behaviour in establishing positive, respectful, leadership and relationships as a teacher. This is an extensive study – in essay form – of the nature of teacher leadership in management and discipline contexts; it is practical, engaging and immediately relevant.

'I've tried being tough on them. I've tried being friendly with them. You know, it really feels like...they couldn't give a damn. At the moment I don't feel there's anything I can do with them at all. They've completely...I've completely lost it with them at the moment. I don't want to speak to them. I don't want to see them. I don't want anything to do with them at the moment...They've let me down so badly.'

Teachers will be familiar with the despairing tone of the newly qualified teacher reflecting on his difficulties with a year 10 class. What he suggests is that there are different ways in which teachers attempt to manage students, or more precisely, different ways in which they present their relationships to students (I've tried being tough...I've tried being friendly...). Unfortunately nothing is working for him. This chapter attempts to describe some of the approaches that teachers use to establish and maintain control, and some of the factors which bear upon the way they respond to disruption in any given situation. It will also consider why these approaches may sometimes fail, as they apparently did for the teacher quoted above.

Different approaches have long been recognised in relation to management of business organisations. Tannenbaum & Schmidt (1958) described approaches ranging from 'Boss-centred leadership', where superiors make decisions and simply announce them, to 'Subordinate-centred leadership', where subordinates are permitted to function and take decisions within the limits defined by the superiors. Rudolph Dreikurs (1982) described similar approaches in teaching, contrasting autocratic and democratic leaders, though he was clearly attempting to portray a 'good guy, bad guy' characterisation to point out the pitfalls of externally imposed control.

Autocratic	**Democratic**
Boss	*Leader*
Sharp voice	*Friendly voice*
Command	*Invitation*
Power	*Influence*
Pressure	*Stimulation*
Demands co-operation	*Wins co-operation*
'I tell you what you should do'	*'I tell you what I would like you to do'*
Imposes ideas	*Sells ideas*
Dominates	*Guides*
Criticises	*Encourages*
Finds fault	*Acknowledges achievement*
Punishes	*Helps*
'I tell you'	*Discusses*
'I decide, you obey'	*'I suggest and help you decide'*
Has sole responsibility of the group	*Shares responsibility of team*

Driekurs (1982)

The negative characteristics of the autocratic style that Dreikurs describes are clearly unacceptable in the current climate that emphasises respect for the rights of young people, and teachers who behave in those ways frequently find themselves in escalating conflicts. Many students are not prepared to accept disrespectful treatment from teachers, and nor should they. Nevertheless, there are occasions when teachers have the responsibility to take control of a situation and Dreikurs recognised that a firm hand was sometimes necessary, but without the personally negative attitudes.

'Combine kindness with firmness. The child must always sense that you are his friend, but that you would not accept certain kinds of behaviour.'

Thomas & Tymon (1985), in discussing modes of handling conflict, describe two underlying dimensions which influence one's behaviour when in conflicts with others: *co-operativeness* – attempting to satisfy the other person's concerns, and *assertiveness*, attempting to satisfy one's own concerns. Figure 1 shows their model relating the two dimensions, which describes five modes of handling conflict.

Competing, i.e. being unco-operative and attempting to win, if necessary using one's powers to force others to concede.

Accommodating, the opposite of competing, i.e. being co-operative and unassertive, seeking to satisfy the other's concerns at the expense of one's own.

Avoiding, i.e. being unco-operative and unassertive, by postponing or not confronting the conflict issue or withdrawing from a threatening situation.

Collaborating, the opposite of avoiding, i.e. being co-operative and assertive, attempting to work with the other person to find a mutually satisfying solution.

Compromising, the intermediate stance for both co-operativeness and assertiveness, attempting to agree on a middle ground solution that offers partial satisfaction to both parties.

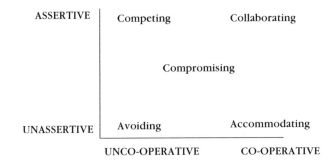

Figure 1. Conflict handling modes

Initially such models were used primarily to identify and recommend collaboration, or problem solving, as the most constructive approach to conflict management. However, the process of collaboration not only requires the other person to co-operate, but is also time-consuming, so when groups of chief executive officers of organisations were asked to identify uses of the conflict handling modes, they generated a list for each one, suggesting that factors such as the time available and the attitudes and knowledge of the people in conflict should be taken into account. For example, competing was considered appropriate '...when decisive action is vital, for example in emergencies; on issues vital to company welfare when you know you are right; when people take advantage of non competitive behaviour.' Avoiding was considered appropriate 'when an issue is trivial or when more important issues are pressing; when you see no chance of satisfying your own concerns; to let people cool down and regain perspective.'

Clearly, the seriousness of the issue in conflict is a major factor influencing the approach used; where there is a great deal at stake, people are more likely to compete.

When people have interests in common they might be expected to work together to resolve the conflict to their mutual benefit, but when their interests differ, they are more likely to compete. Figure 2 shows these two dimensions in relation to the five approaches, suggested by Thomas and Tymon.

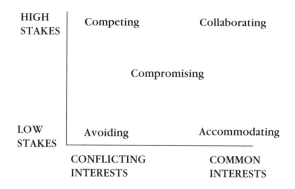

Figure 2. Conflict handling modes

The conflicts for chief executive officers dealing with their subordinates are similar to those facing teachers dealing with challenging students, though their powers differ, and in different situations teachers may also need to adopt different approaches. What approaches, therefore, might teachers adopt in response to challenging behaviour from students and what factors are likely to affect the appropriateness of a particular approach?

THE BOSS, THE MANAGER AND THE LEADER

To return to the description by Dreikurs of the autocratic 'Boss' and the democratic 'Leader': *competing* is clearly a major feature of the former, whereas the latter could encompass *collaborating, compromising* and even *accommodating*, as they all involve trying to work with, rather than against student offenders. *Avoiding* could also be a feature of a democratic approach provided that the avoidance is 'tactical' (Rogers 1998) – that is, it is a deliberate decision by the teacher to overlook a minor distraction or a transient offence or to defer dealing with a serious one until a more suitable time. On the other hand, if teachers avoid intervening or accommodate to the wishes of the student because they are uncertain as to what action to take, or are anxious about confronting students, then they are not in control of the situation. This will be discussed later.

In addition to the approaches of 'Boss' and 'Leader', a further distinction can be made which represents a neutral position between these two extremes, neither working against, nor working with the offender, but acting officially and impersonally in the role of 'Manager'.

When responding to unwanted behaviour as the Boss, competing with offending students and attempting to take control, the major emphasis of the teacher's intervention is the condemnation of the behaviour. Teachers must not show negative attitudes towards the student but must be absolutely clear about the unacceptability of the student's *action*, and show the determination to correct it: e.g. **confronting, determined, insistent, forceful, resolute.** Unfortunately, some teachers responding in these ways unwittingly express personally negative attitudes such as demanding, threatening, intimidating, blaming and berating behaviours, which reveal a dislike and disregard for the student, and this can lead to escalating confrontations and worsening relationships between teacher and student(s).

As the democratic Leader, the major emphasis is on showing regard for the students. The teacher still shows disapproval of their actions, but in a more benign way, which carries an implication that they can be expected to correct their own behaviour: e.g. **tolerant, reasonable, disapproving, disappointed, concerned or serious.** In this way teachers express a closeness and trust in the relationship, and an expectation that the students will co-operate.

When responding to offences as the Manager the manner must reflect the neutrality of the teacher, as one who has the professional responsibility to enforce the rules and maintain order, but without being personally involved with the student, or in judgement of their behaviour: e.g. **businesslike, professional, confident, impartial, respectful, assertive and decisive**.

FACTORS INFLUENCING ONE'S APPROACH WHEN INTERVENING IN STUDENTS' BEHAVIOUR

Most teachers hope to get to know their students well and to develop co-operative relationships so that when an intervention is necessary, it can be managed (wherever possible) in low-key ways, consistent with being the Leader. These 'reminders' are usually private and covert, implying a sense of solidarity with the students and a wish not to embarrass them in front of their peers. They are usually carried out incidentally so that the ongoing activity is not interrupted, and other students do not notice the teacher's action. For example, while speaking to the class the teacher moves near to two students who are quietly talking or gestures to another to put a packet of crisps away. Such low-key interventions convey the expectation that students will co-operate when reminded about their behaviour and, by avoiding more public and intrusive interventions, teachers promote and foster trust in their relationships.

The problem arises when such measures are either inappropriate, or when students fail to co-operate, e.g.:

▶ if the students have very hostile attitudes towards the teacher or towards authority in general

▶ if the teacher's relationship with the students is in its very early stages so that there is little basis for the expression of trust. In these circumstances some students might view these private messages from teachers as weak, attempting to avoid a confrontation, or as manipulative, implying a close relationship simply to gain compliance

▶ if the disruptive or offensive behaviours are attention-seeking and are being reinforced by the teacher's benign intervention

▶ if the offences are serious, such as aggressive or abusive behaviour or vandalising property

▶ if the offences are dangerous and require immediate and decisive action from the teacher

▶ if there is general disorder in the classroom.

In some of the above circumstances, therefore, it may be necessary for teachers to follow up with a more intrusive approach or even to do so in the first instance.

Figure 3 shows a possible relationship between the persistence or seriousness of the offences (high stakes, low stakes) and various factors which can be significant in influencing the manner in which teachers intervene.

Co-operativeness

A major factor in teacher leadership is whether or not the students might be expected to co-operate with the teacher. In some cases, the teacher and student will have common interests (e.g. they both wish the student to do well in an examination) so the student would be responsive to a friendly reminder. On the other hand, some behaviour is clearly intended to involve other students in disruption or is carried out publicly as a direct challenge to, or disregard for, the teacher's authority. In such circumstances it would be incongruous to respond in ways which expressed trust unless the behaviour was suddenly uncharacteristic from a normally co-operative student.

Context

If we can speak to a student privately, it allows us to show concern and understanding, even though it may be necessary to administer consequences. The aim should be to improve the relationship with the student, or at least not to worsen it. Taking offending students aside and speaking quietly and privately to them, or arranging to see them during breaks or lunchtimes, gives teachers the

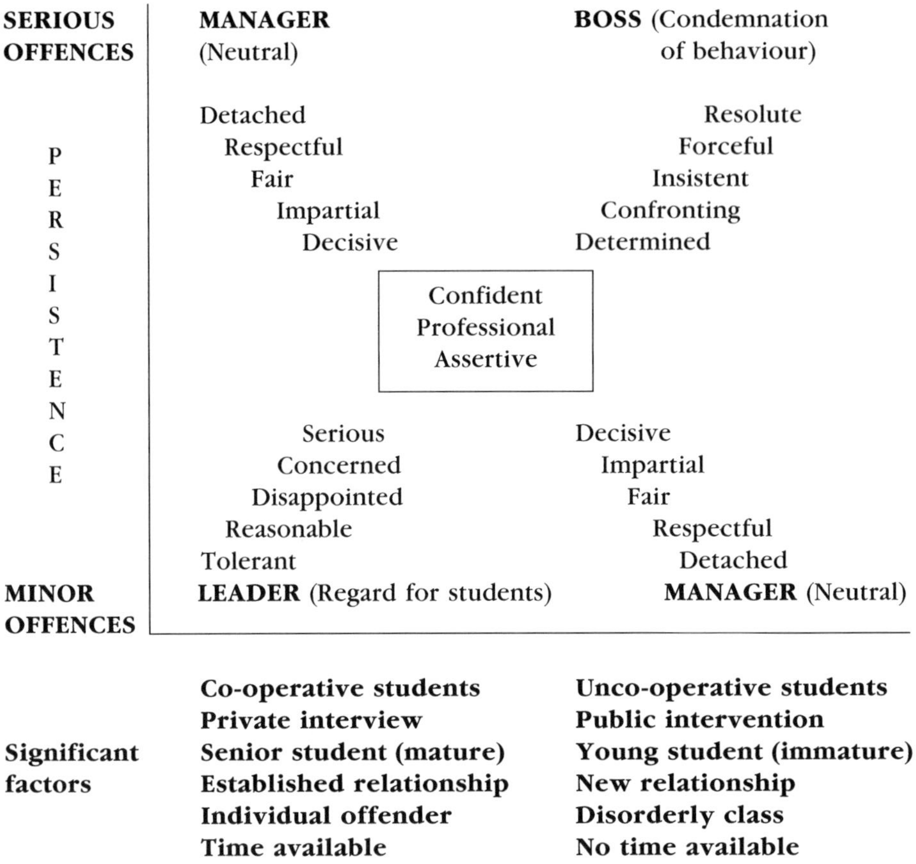

SERIOUS OFFENCES	MANAGER (Neutral)	BOSS (Condemnation of behaviour)
P E R S I S T E N C E	Detached Respectful Fair Impartial Decisive	Resolute Forceful Insistent Confronting Determined
	Confident Professional Assertive	
	Serious Concerned Disappointed Reasonable Tolerant	Decisive Impartial Fair Respectful Detached
MINOR OFFENCES	LEADER (Regard for students)	MANAGER (Neutral)

Significant factors	Co-operative students Private interview Senior student (mature) Established relationship Individual offender Time available	Unco-operative students Public intervention Young student (immature) New relationship Disorderly class No time available

Figure 3. Factors affecting responses to students' disorder

opportunity to express more personal, less 'professional' relationships. How-ever, in public settings, teachers frequently need to be *seen* to act firmly and decisively in response to unwanted behaviour, to show everyone that the behaviour is unacceptable and will not be tolerated. A more professional response is therefore likely to be necessary when intervening publicly, though the action taken might be to see the students privately later.

Maturity

Teachers must consider whether students are mature enough to understand the significance of their actions and will not misinterpret a tactful or covert intervention as avoidance. If young children learn that teachers will avoid dealing firmly with their challenges it becomes increasingly difficult to do so as they grow older. When faced with unreasonable, persistent or serious behaviour from young and immature children it may sometimes be necessary for teachers to adopt insistent and resolute approaches and to give behaviour-consequences, to encourage them to be accountable for their actions. More mature students are likely to respond to a reasoned or professional approach.

Length of relationship

Trust takes time to develop, and in the very early meetings with a class it is therefore more appropriate to correct behaviour in formal ways which emphasise the 'professional' nature of the relationships. As we get to know students individually it is then consistent to express more friendly, almost protective, attitudes which reflect and foster the personal aspects of the relationship but which also disapprove of the behaviour. All teachers will be familiar with the advice not to be too friendly at the outset and not to 'smile till Christmas', which warn against over-familiarity with students too soon. However, relationships are now much more informal and in the course of normal teaching, when students are co-operating, it is important for teachers to relax from the outset and to show a personal interest in them, and an enjoyment of the lessons. When correcting behaviour, however, a more detached, professional manner gives an unambiguous message to the student.

Size of group

When there is general disorder with a larger group of students, so that at any one time there are several talking or calling out and others out of their seats or otherwise off task, one's priority is to re-establish order. It is a mistake to try to intervene with individual students against a background of disorder, to make them sit down, resume work or move seat. The less one has to do to restore order, the better. Teachers who can achieve this simply by appearing at the classroom door with a look which conveys 'What do you think you're doing?' rely upon their well-established authority, and at the same time reinforce it, but in some instances it may be necessary to be more active. Achieving 'crowd control' involves persistent, unambiguous and insistent behaviour from teachers, leaving students in no doubt that they mean what they say and are in control of themselves and the situation. It may be necessary, therefore, to raise one's voice above the noise to gain attention, and then to insist that order is restored by repeating instructions in a calm, definite, uncompromising manner. Acting as the Boss in this way is not directed specifically at any one individual, though names may sometimes be used, so it is less likely to generate indignant or hostile reactions from students.

Time available

In the Elton Report (DES, 1989), the strategy that was rated as the most effective in dealing with difficult classes or pupils by the largest proportion of teachers was 'reasoning with a pupil or pupils outside the classroom setting'. Desirable as reasoning may be, teachers have limited time to engage in lengthy discussions in the day-to-day dealing with disruptions in the classroom, so they should aim to spend as little time as possible explaining and justifying their actions to offenders, so as not to encroach on valuable teaching time. If one can put aside time during breaks or after lesson time to speak to students about their behaviour, not to chastise but to try to improve the situation, this might result in fewer problems in the long run. Rather than using a detention to deter behaviour by chastising, or setting an arduous or boring task, the time would be better spent in trying to reason with the students to try to fix the problem, following the agenda 'What happened? Why is it a problem? What are we going to do about it? What will happen if it continues?' (Robertson 1996,1997). The stated aim of such discussions would be to put right the problem in question, but the underlying aim should be to try to improve the relationship with the student. This is more likely to be achieved by keeping the meeting informal and showing interest in, and concern for the student, even though one may still have to give fair consequences for the offence. There is, of course, no guarantee that any approach, no matter how reasonable, will improve one's relationships with students. Their problems and attitudes may be deeply entrenched, or they may not respond to the personal characteristics of particular teachers (such as age, gender, or personality). One may have to settle for not generating further animosity and worsening the relationship, which is often the outcome of a disciplinary interview.

The relationship between the above factors and the teacher's action, as set out in Figure 3, can clearly not be definitive and in most circumstances one should err on the side of the more tolerant and reasonable approach of the Leader, implying a co-operative relationship with the student. For example, consider these extracts transcribed from videotaped teaching.

The teacher knows the year 8 class well but, untypically, two girls are covertly talking and looking at a note while he is explaining a problem to the class. He stops briefly in mid-sentence and looks in their direction. They look up, noticing the silence, to see the teacher raise his eyebrows with a questioning expression which conveys 'I'm surprised at you', before continuing with his explanation. Later, the class are quietly working but the same two girls are again chattering and giggling. The teacher moves near to within a foot or so and looks directly at the girls who by this time are looking back in a smiling, slightly embarrassed way. 'Emma, Tracey...' (he says quietly, not drawing attention to them), 'what is it with you two today? Is there something in the water?' They giggle nervously and one says, 'Sorry sir... we are doing the work.' He looks at their books. 'I can see you've made a start but I think you'd get on a lot better if you worked on your own, don't you?' The teacher then moves away and although they remain together, they work quietly for the rest of the lesson.

The low-key, non-verbal intervention, followed by the private, informal word, humorously suggesting that an external agent was causing their behaviour, and then leaving them with the responsibility to put things right, all reflected and reinforced the Leader relationship of trust with the students. On occasions when students do not co-operate, teachers can follow up with a more formal, managerial approach, calmly and firmly telling one of the students to move.

In some extreme circumstances such as dealing with a rowdy class or dangerous behaviour, the teacher may need to take control quickly, which will call for the determination and insistence of the Boss.

EARNING AUTHORITY

Why is it then that some classes seem to be beyond the teacher's control? The reality is usually that only a small number of students in a class are effectively out of control, but they are able to disrupt the teaching and set the tone for the rest of the class. When there is general disorder in the room, with students wandering around, calling to one another, and the teacher either passively ignoring them or desperately trying to establish order, it is not surprising that even normally well-behaved students get drawn into the disruption. When teachers fail to take control, democracy does not ensue; the door is left open for irresponsible students to step in and take over. Once this has happened the teacher will find it very difficult to re-assert his or her authority with the class, as any approach, whether it be as the Boss, Manager or Leader, will be resisted by those students who have taken over.

Authority is essentially an agreement between the teacher and students and without this, teachers do not have sufficient powers to wrest control from the ringleaders to enforce order. Rogers (1997) has described ways in which authority can be re-negotiated with a class but it is preferable to make sure one establishes it securely in the first place. This does not mean that one should be harsh and heartless, vigorously clamping down on any sign of dissent; successful teachers treat students with respect from the outset and quickly earn the authority they claim by teaching in a stimulating and committed way. Figure 4 shows the bases which justify or legitimise a teacher's claim to the relationships of Boss, Manager and Leader.

As the Manager, the 'credentials' which form the basis for one's claim to be in a professional relationship with the student are predominantly one's pedagogic expertise and subject knowledge. Jacob Kounin (1970), in his research into classroom management, demonstrated that disruption occurred mainly when students were waiting, either physically, not having the knowledge or resources to get on with the task, or intellectually, because the lesson or tasks lacked challenge or stimulation: putting it more simply, because they were bored. At such times students found their own ways of filling in the time or enlivening the proceedings, and Kounin, in his conclusions, stressed the importance of efficient organisation and planning in avoiding such occasions.

> '...the business of running a classroom is a complicated technology having to do with developing a nonsatiating learning program; programming for progress, challenge, and variety in learning activities; initiating and maintaining movement in classroom tasks with smoothness and momentum; coping with more than one event simultaneously; observing and emitting feedback for many different events; directing actions at appropriate targets; maintaining focus upon a group; and doubtless other techniques not measured in these researches.' (Kounin 1970)

Good subject knowledge is also vital for the teacher to be able to assess students' comprehension by asking the right questions to explore their conceptual development and lead them to a better understanding. Asking challenging questions and providing appropriate activities are essential to stimulate and maintain students' motivation.

EXPRESSING ATTITUDES

When problems do arise, the ability to exercise authority convincingly requires personal qualities such as confidence, assertiveness and decisiveness. These are attitudes that are easily recognised but much more difficult to describe as there are subtleties in the communication which are crucial and can easily be overlooked when attempting to convey these impressions. Of equal or greater significance than the words one uses are the vocal or prosodic features of one's speech. Variations in tone, pitch, volume and timing, coupled with facial expressions and contextual aspects such as status differences, all convey subtle differences in meaning. For example, when giving an instruction about behaviour, reminding a student to attend, a teacher might say, 'Mark... (waits for eye-contact) Could you put that down and pay attention please.' By waiting for the student to look back at you before continuing, it is more likely that he will be attending and be fully aware of the non-verbal aspects of the message, such as your facial expression. If one raises one's eyebrows when speaking to the student, this has two functions. Firstly, it is an 'eyes wide open' attention signal (I am attending to you) and secondly it is non-threatening. If in any doubt, the reader should adopt a knitted-brow, threatening frown, then raise the eyebrows: the threat disappears. The teacher should also not be moving around when giving the instruction as this detracts from the focused nature of the message.

The first such instruction is further mitigated or 'softened' by such measures as using a request form and adding 'please' (French & Peskett 1986). It is still perceived as an instruction and not a question because of the tone of voice and the fact that it is the teacher saying it, but if one's authority is in question, a challenging student might well exploit the ambiguity of the 'request' to attend by

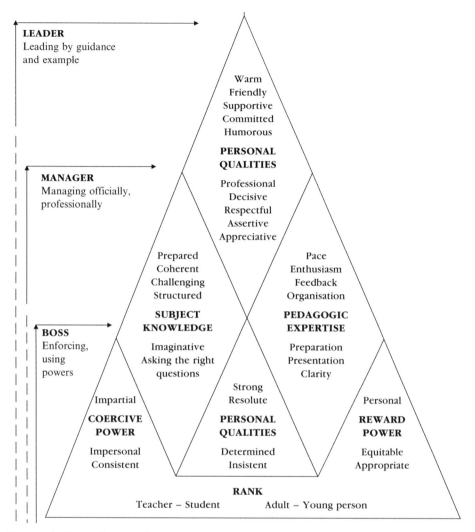

Figure 4. Bases for teacher–student relationships

replying 'Yeah, in a minute', or even 'No, I'm busy'. Teachers use mitigated forms of instructions probably because they give students the opportunity to co-operate, which is not possible when one is given an imperative or command; one can then only obey or disobey, e.g. 'Put that down and pay attention'.

The intonation of the instruction is also of considerable significance in conveying, sometimes unintentionally, one's intentions and feelings. Different dialects have characteristic intonations and one cannot necessarily associate a particular pattern with a specific attitude. Nevertheless, some emotions and intentions are easily recognised. Frustration is conveyed by a sharp, audible intake of breath before speaking, a pained facial expression, 'roller coaster' variations in pitch, and vocal emphasis on syllables in key words e.g.

MAAARRK WOULD YOU PLEASE PAY ATTENTION

(*Variations in the pitch, not volume, are indicated by the relative height of the letters.*) Such a wits' end, whining delivery would make very little impression on most students as it acknowledges a lack of power and authority in the relationship. In contrast, a stepped rise in pitch of about a tone on the final syllables carries a sense of expectation that the instruction will be followed; an unresolved chord that will be completed by the student's compliance, e.g.

COULD YOU PUT THAT DOWN AND PAY ATTENTION THANKS

Rogers (1994) recommends the use of 'thanks' instead of 'please' as he points out that this implies you expect students to co-operate. It also further emphasises that it is not a request but a polite instruction.

The features of a firmly delivered, non-confrontational 'managerial' instruction are therefore:

▶ making sure the student is attending, preferably giving eye-contact
▶ using a 'brow-raise' and expectant expression
▶ speaking with a level pitch which rises at the end of the instruction
▶ using 'thanks' rather than 'please'
▶ standing still.

The intonation used for informal, genuine requests such as asking for the salt to be passed at the dinner table, usually rises in pitch on the key word or stressed syllable at the end of the sentence, and ends in a relative fall in pitch on the word 'please', e.g.

COULD YOU PASS THE SALT PLEASE

This polite request form might therefore seem inappropriate for an instruction, but it is often used by teachers, e.g.

COULD YOU PUT THAT AWAY NOW PLEASE

However, the fact that teachers' 'requests' concern students' *behaviour* implies they have the right to intervene and can expect students to comply. The use of such mitigated 'control instructions' has been widely observed at primary and secondary levels, so would seem to be common practice, at least for the first instruction (Holmes 1983; French & Peskett 1986). Given that teachers have established the Leader role, students can certainly be expected to co-operate with this polite, invitational form of instruction and, in so doing, reinforce the relationship of mutual trust.

In contrast, as the 'Boss', the teacher needs to make it clear that the student must take the instruction seriously, so there is no attempt to soften or mitigate the delivery. The request form is not used, nor are 'please' or 'thanks', and there is a stepped fall in pitch at the end of the sentence, giving the impression that no other options are available, e.g.

GIVE ME THE RULER NOW

NOW TAKE YOUR BOOK AND WORK OVER AT THE SIDE

When speaking to an individual student in this way, extra care must be taken to appear respectful and firm, but non-confrontational, so the instruction should be delivered in a quiet, controlled manner and as privately as possible.

Pitfalls

When we intervene in students' behaviour and ask questions which identify the offence: 'Why are you (writing; talking; out of your seat)?' or 'What are you (giggling about; fiddling with; looking out of the window for)?' we invite them to give reasons, which can lead to unnecessary protracted exchanges. Rogers (1994) recommends that one should instead ask a 'What' question, (Jason . . . What are you doing?'), so that one can then redirect them back to the required activity after their reply, e.g. 'I'm just copying the notes.' 'Fine, could you leave that now and give me your attention, thanks'. Good & Brophy (1978) also pointed out that 'Why', and similar questions, are usually asked in a whining or critical tone and are, in fact, attacks on students. Teachers are not really asking questions but are criticising or complaining about the student's behaviour. This inclines them to deny or defend their actions. Neutral questions, ('What are you doing?', 'Is there a problem?', 'Do you need any help?'), allow the teacher to follow-up by redirecting the student to the required activity.

Another pitfall for teachers is the tendency to elaborate on an instruction or to pose it as a sarcastic hint. This provides outspoken or challenging students with the opportunity to exploit the ambiguity and turn the tables on the teacher, as the following examples show.

▶ Some students are chattering while the teacher is addressing the class. 'How many teachers are there in this classroom?' Students start counting each other, pointedly leaving the teacher out.

▶ A student is gazing out of the window while the teacher works through a problem on the blackboard. 'Kevin . . . which direction is the blackboard?' Students start calling out suggestions for the direction, and one shouts 'Anyone got a compass?'

▶ The students are individually working on a task, as the teacher walks round helping. Some students are chattering. 'I can hear you talking. I've got eyes in the back of my head.' Someone calls out 'Yeah, bug eyes.' Other students jeer.

The first two examples would not pose a problem for a teacher in a Leader relationship with a class, and might even momentarily enliven the proceedings with the shared joke. The teacher would be able to restore order quickly. In early meetings with a class, however – before a relationship of trust has been reached – teachers would be advised to keep the interventions brief, to the point and, if possible, private. In the last example, the scornful attitude expressed towards the teacher shows that, in making such a remark, he had misjudged his relationship, at least with some of the students. A teacher would not be able to share in such a 'joke', or even passively accept it, being the object of the ridicule; he would only appear weak and out of control. Even attempts to react firmly to such remarks can degenerate into a display of frustration and anger if the students do not comply. A teacher in control would be far less likely to receive such a response, or to have other students join in, and would also be able to react calmly and firmly if such rudeness did occur. It is better to discuss such incidents privately later, not to chastise the student, but to make it clear that such remarks are unacceptable.

THE BOSS: RESPECTFUL BUT RESOLUTE

Supporting the teacher's claim to be the Manager are the ascribed powers to reward and coerce by virtue of their 'rank' in relation to students, and these form the basis of one's claim to be the Boss. When students challenge a teacher's managerial role, the teacher may need to exercise these powers fairly and appropriately, and also show the determination to do so.

When faced with an unco-operative student, it is important to appear relaxed and completely in control of oneself and of the situation. In the following extract, transcribed from video, Graham, a year 10 student, has been fooling around with his partner seated beside him at a table, but has refused to move seat when told to do so by the class teacher. She sends for the deputy head. As she enters from the door at the back of the room the teacher tells her that Graham has been fooling around and has refused to move his seat. She moves behind and to the side of Graham, standing about two feet away and looking down at him. Her arm is lifted towards him, intervening with an open-hand palm-down gesture. He is aware of her but looks down and fiddles with a pen.

'Graham . . . Graham . . . (as she speaks he points to his partner.) 'He started it.' (She continues.) 'Graham. Stop messing about with that, look at me.'

(As Graham, head still down and propped up on his arm, turns to look at her, she continues.) 'Come on get yourself out to the room.' (As she speaks she steps back and to the side, indicating the path to the door by motioning with her outstretched arm. Graham immediately gets up and walks past her to the door and she follows.)

Throughout the incident, which took only 30 seconds, the deputy head looked relaxed, with a neutral, non-threatening facial expression, and spoke calmly and quietly to the student. One could argue that the boy complied because he was dealing with the deputy head teacher, which was, of course, significant. However, her behaviour was consistent with his perception of her rank, as she appeared entirely confident that she could manage the situation. The focused attention, the quiet insistence that he should look at her, the use of unmitigated imperatives, all gave the impression that the student did not have any alternative but to follow her instruction. Her intonation did not have the informal friendliness of the Leader giving advice, or the final rising expectancy of the Manager, inviting co-operation; instead there was a lowering of pitch on the final words 'that', 'me' and 'room' which conveyed that compliance was understood; the game with the class teacher was over. Had the class teacher approached Graham with the same sense of calm certainty, he might have moved his seat.

'Graham . . . (waits for eye contact) I gave you a choice . . . now take your books and work over at the side.'

When it is necessary to give such firm instructions one should then move away, conveying an expectation that the student will comply. It is also easier for students to move without losing face if the teacher is not standing over them and appearing to be forcing them to move. When students fail to comply with firmly stated instructions, the school behaviour policy must set out procedures to support teachers, to ensure that students are held accountable for their actions.

APPRECIATING STUDENTS' EFFORTS

The power to 'reward' is, of course, a feature of all three approaches, but as the Leader, the reward 'value' rests primarily in the personal positive reaction from the respected teacher rather than in any additional token or merit. The most status-enhancing praise is an unqualified appreciation of the student's contribution or effort, conveyed in the teacher's reaction, with or without the use of superlatives. Consider how a teacher might simply repeat a student's answer, say, 'It gets heavier when it burns', to convey:

> 'That took you long enough. I thought it would never sink in.'
> 'Yes, that's right.'
> 'Yes, you've got it!'

Appreciation of a student's efforts involves a positive personal reaction from the teacher which conveys, 'You've done something that . . . I admire; I am grateful for; surprises me' rather than the unemotional, 'I'm going to say something to make *you* feel pleased . . . Well done.'

Why is *unqualified* appreciation a status-enhancing experience for students? Imagine you have gone to a great deal of trouble to prepare a special meal for your spouse or partner. He or she eats the meal with relish and after consuming the last morsel from the plate says 'That was delicious. That sauce was so tasty. See what you can do when you really try? Now if you could only keep the kitchen a little tidier . . .' How often do we detract from an appreciative reaction by re-asserting our teacher role with similar qualifying remarks? When a student has made an effort to co-operate, a quiet private word of appreciation from the teacher (e.g. 'You came up with some really excellent suggestions Paul.') is better without the qualification 'See what you can do when you don't fool around all the time?'

REVEALING ONE'S LACK OF CONTROL

The basis for one's claim to be the Leader depends primarily on the personal relationship of trust and mutual respect, but it is supported by the firm foundations of one's professional skills and ascribed powers. Respect for and trust in teachers will not develop if they are disorganised, have weak subject knowledge and lack the personal qualities to relate well to students. The best such teachers can hope for is pity, though they are more likely to receive contempt. Similarly, if students are to accept that teachers sometimes need to assert their authority firmly as the Boss, they must trust and respect them. Teachers who have weak professional skills and show little regard for students will not be able to rely on their limited ascribed powers to establish authority, nor should they expect the support of a whole school behaviour policy without making every effort to improve.

Figure 5 describes the 'Recipe for failure' where the teacher lacks the personal qualities and professional skills, and exercises the powers inappropriately. In such unacceptable circumstances, teachers are unable to use any approach effectively and will fail to establish their authority. The time-consuming priority for senior colleagues is then to help them improve their skills and restore order without further alienating the students.

The newly qualified teacher quoted at the beginning of this chapter was required to teach Personal and Social Education in his first lesson with his year 10 tutor group, a subject for which he was not trained. In spite of his best efforts, his subject knowledge was shown to be lacking when unexpected facts were needed and, being inexperienced, his pedagogic skills were weak. After a short, inadequate introduction to the topic he distributed worksheets and set the class into discussion groups of four or five students. He sat with one group to participate in the discussion. One boy, in full view of the teacher, began to fold his worksheet to make a paper aeroplane, an action which called for a managerial intervention from the new teacher, such as, 'Can you straighten that out thanks, I'll be collecting them in later.' or 'Could you not fold that up thanks, we'll be using it this lesson.' What he actually said was, 'Hey...that took me...two seconds to photocopy that.' This tentative hint, trying to make a joke of the intervention, reflected his uncertainty about the relationship he should establish with the students; a fear of causing offence; of being disliked; of being disregarded.

Imagine a very different context. A teacher has prepared a paper for a staff working party. He sits with the small group of teachers around a table in the staff-room and distributes the photocopied paper. One teacher begins to fold up his copy into a piece of origami. Would it then be appropriate to say, 'Could you not fold that up thanks, we'll be using it later'? In such circumstances a remark like that to a colleague would seem overbearing and would probably be responded to in a 'Who do you think you are talking to?' manner. One would be far more likely to do nothing about it or to intervene in a friendly way with a joking hint like 'Hey...that took me two seconds to photocopy that'. When the

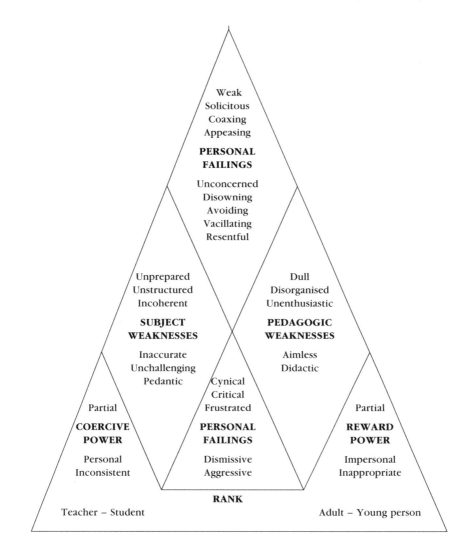

Figure 5. Recipe for failure

teacher intervened in this weak, hesitant way with the student, it is not surprising that the latter then flight-tested his creation; the very thing the teacher wished to avoid.

In the first meeting with this class, therefore, not only was his weak subject knowledge exposed, but his inexperience led him to be tentative and solicitous in his attempts to manage the students' behaviour. In subsequent lessons the more challenging students quickly became bolder, and their behaviour more extreme, forcing the teacher to try to regain control.

'Can you stop it! (banging the student's table) You're driving me round the twist! . . . Pack it in . . . The pair of you can sit in here all night . . . Stop fidgeting with each other and messing about!'

What was clearly an attempt to 'be tough' became an expression of his own frustration at being unable to control the students' behaviour. Instead of feeling intimidated and chastened by this emotional display, many of the students sniggered excitedly or openly laughed at his loss of self-control.

In Figure 3 there were examples of attitudes which expressed a measure of control by the teacher, such as concern, confidence, and insistence. In contrast, when students are in control, teachers express attitudes that reveal their failure to cope.

▶ Futile attempts to be the Leader ('I've tried being friendly') result in weakly accommodating to the students' behaviour to avoid confrontations, or compliant, appeasing attitudes in the hope of being liked ('that took me two seconds to photocopy that')

▶ At the other extreme, futile and negative efforts to be the Boss ('I've tried being tough') can result in frustration and anger when students oppose the teacher's attempts to gain control ('you're driving me round the twist').

▶ Attempts to remain neutral and detached are difficult to sustain and can result in teachers passively disowning the problems beyond their control ('I don't want anything to do with them at the moment').

Below are some typical examples of unhelpful attitudes that, when expressed, do nothing to restore order but simply reveal one's impotence. A teacher may have recourse to some or all to these misguided efforts to regain control in a single lesson with a single student, but more likely with a group who are effectively stopping any teaching or learning taking place.

Appeasing/complaisant/non-assertive ('I want them to care about me.')
Avoiding, tentative, cajoling, pleading, anxious

Disowning ('They don't care about me, so I don't care about them.')
Passive, unconcerned, ignoring, dismissive, rejecting

Victimised ('They're just impossible!')
Reproachful, critical, accusing, frustrated, angry

GENERAL PRINCIPLES FOR INTERVENTIONS

This chapter has described various ways in which teachers intervene to correct behaviour, but regardless of the approach used, there are some general principles that can be drawn in summary.

▶ Whenever possible, err on the side of low-key interventions that present co-operative relationships with students.

▶ Show regard for students, or at the very least, respect.
▶ Try to keep interventions as private as possible.
▶ Try to remain calm and avoid revealing unhelpful feelings.
▶ Always follow up on any unresolved problem.
▶ Defer dealing with situations that are likely to encroach on your teaching time.
▶ Try to improve your relationships with students, or at least not worsen them.

Finally, we must keep a sense of perspective about the problems which students present to us, and about our capacity to solve them rather than cope with them. Relatively speaking, as problems go, they are mostly not that serious, but they can be very wearing on a day-to-day basis if we fail to cope. Perhaps we should bear in mind that – as Abraham Lincoln might have put it –

Some of the students will co-operate all of the time,
and all of the students will co-operate some of the time,
but all of the students will not co-operate all of the time.

REFERENCES

DES (1989) *Discipline in Schools* (The Elton Report), London: HMSO.
Dreikurs, R. (1982) *Maintaining Sanity in the Classroom,* New York: Harper & Row.
French and Peskett (1986) Control Instructions in the Infant Classroom, *Educational Research* 28, 3, 210–19.
Good & Brophy (1978) *Looking in Classrooms* (2nd edn.), New York: Harper & Row.
Holmes, J. (1983) 'The structures of teachers' directives' in Richards, J. C. and Schmidt, R. W. (eds.) *Language and Communication,* London & New York: Longman.
Kounin, J. S. (1970) *Discipline and Group Management in Classrooms.* New York: Holt, Rinehart & Winston.
Robertson, J. (1996) *Effective Classroom Control* (3rd edn.) London: Hodder & Stoughton.
Robertson, J. (1997) *No Need to Shout.* Oxford: Ginn Heinemann.
Rogers, B. (1994) *The Language of Discipline.* Plymouth: Northcote House.
Rogers, B. (1997) *Cracking the Hard Class.* London: Paul Chapman. (In Australia Sydney: Scholastic Books.)
Rogers, B. (1998) *You Know the Fair Rule.* London: Paul Chapman. (In Australia Melbourne: ACER Press.)
Tannenbaum, R. & Schmidt, W. H. (1973) How to choose a leadership pattern, *Harvard Business Review* May/June 162–180.
Thomas, K. W. & Tymon, W. G. (1985) Structural Approaches to Conflict Management in Tannenbaum, R. *et al Human Systems Development*, San Francisco: Jossey Boss Inc.

3

A humanistic view of discipline

Chris Kyriacou

Discipline and effective teaching are essential to order in class-room life and learning. Chris Kyriacou argues that the kind of discipline we exercise is crucial to effective learning and supportive relationships. Within the humanistic paradigm, Chris sets out the features and characteristics of 'good discipline' for teacher-leaders. He consistently emphasises the need for authority based on, and in, effective teaching and quality relationships. There is the underlying, axiomatic emphasis on respect for pupils in a teacher's management practice. The emphasis on teacher skill is developed with specific and wide-ranging examples of how a teacher can be preventative, proactive, appropriately corrective and 'punitive' as well as necessarily supportive.

Discipline in the classroom can be described as the order necessary to enable teaching and learning to proceed effectively. All classrooms must have discipline. There is no way that a teacher would be able to ensure that pupils were engaged in the learning activities unless there was sufficient leadership control over what happens during the lesson. However, one of the greatest mistakes a new teacher can make is to think that discipline is something they exert that is different from their general teaching. By this I mean to say that it is easy for a new teacher to think there are two sides to being a teacher in the classroom – one side involves teaching about the topic of the lesson, and the other side involves exerting discipline when pupils misbehave. In these circumstances, as soon as a teacher sees a pupil misbehaving, they flip over from 'teaching mode' into 'discipline mode'. Such a view of how to maintain discipline is an absolute disaster.

The golden rule of maintaining discipline is to realise that good discipline is a natural consequence of good teaching. If we teach effectively by making the work clear and interesting and helping pupils to stay 'on task' by keeping them involved in the lesson and helping them when they have problems with the work, we will find that discipline will follow. If, however, we adopt a 'Jekyll and Hyde' approach to discipline, we will quickly find that we are having to deal with conflicts more and more often with less and less success, which may make us start to consider whether teaching is the right career for us. Maintaining discipline is in a large measure a by-product of good teaching. If a problem arises in the classroom, and we notice a pupil is misbehaving, ask what has led up to the pupil misbehaving. Is the pupil stuck, bored, confused, tired, finding the pace too fast or too slow, worried about failing, or simply unsure of what they should be doing? If we can deal with their problem 'swiftly', and get the pupil back to work quickly, then discipline will be re-established without the need for a 'discipline problem' even having to be acknowledged. Even better, if we can start to identify the warning signs that misbehaviour is about to start, we may even pre-empt the problem occurring before it develops.

RELATIONSHIPS

The key to maintaining good discipline is to establish a good relationship with pupils based on mutual respect and rapport (Cooper and McIntyre, 1996; Morgan and Morris, 1999; Pollard *et al*, 2000). This involves us showing respect for our pupils, by treating them in a polite and courteous manner, and not resorting to making unfair and hurtful comments based on sarcasm or belittling the pupil. At the same time, pupils – ideally – should show respect towards the teacher. This means being courteous and polite towards their teacher, paying attention and 'sitting up properly', following instructions and listening attentively when the teacher is speaking. It is therefore important that the teacher picks up on instances when pupils are behaving in a discourteous manner. Rapport refers to the importance of teachers being able to show they 'get on' with pupils by being able to communicate with them in an authentic manner to convey they are 'on the same wavelength'. Making a comment about the results of a local sports event, the school concert, the weather, whether a pupil is feeling better after having a cold, all indicate how the teacher and pupil can feel comfortable in each other's company on a personal level. Displaying a thoughtful and positive sense of humour is often regarded by pupils as a key indicator of good rapport.

The teacher also, however, needs to be able to command authority. However, this authority should not be based on pupils' fear of the teacher's 'nastier' side. Rather, it should come from the feeling of trust and respect that the pupils have in the manner in which the teacher characteristically exercises their teacher role. In the same way that we all voluntarily accept a tour guide's authority to show us around a new city by doing what they say, so the pupil needs to have trust and confidence that if they co-operate with their teacher that will, likely, result in their educational progress.

Establishing such authority will be easier if we behave as someone who confidently has authority. If we can act with firmness and confidence in our dealings with pupils, then they will come to accept our authority as a natural state of affairs. This requires us to act assertively; looking and sounding relaxed; standing 'upright' and centre stage; circulating around the room freely and with confidence; and making good use of eye contact. If we notice disrespect, we pick up on this (for example), staring sternly at the pupil or asking the pupil to behave appropriately (e.g. 'pay attention please').

PRE-EMPTIVE STRATEGIES

One of the most important skills a teacher needs to develop is vigilance (Dean, 1996; Kyriacou, 1998; Robertson, 1996). This involves continually monitoring what pupils are doing – are they paying attention; doing the work; stuck or confused; talking to another pupil inappropriately when they should be working? A very important part of this skill is to be proactive. We need to distribute our questions around the room to check who is understanding what. When someone is not paying attention, ask them a question about the topic in hand to draw them back to being involved quickly without making a discipline incident out of the event. When pupils are working in their exercise books, circulate around the room and check how they are getting on, how much work they are doing and give help or more stretching tasks where appropriate.

Of course, even with good teaching, good relationships and good use of pre-emptive strategies, misbehaviour will still occur from time to time. However, my main point is that if we get these right, then misbehaviour will normally be kept to a minimum. If we consciously notice that disruption and misbehaviour is more frequent, and disturbing, in our classes it will help to reflect on our characteristic teaching practice, pre-emptive strategies and our relationship with the class group. This is in preference to resorting to more reprimands and punishments.

If we are satisfied, however, that our teaching, relationships and use of pre-emptive strategies are in good health, then in order to maintain discipline we will also have to make appropriate use of two other strategies. The first of these I refer to as 'investigating and counselling' and the second as 'reprimanding'. I see these as operating in parallel. In some cases, the former is more appropriate, and in other cases it is the latter. Part of developing our skill as a teacher is knowing better how to make the right choice at the right time.

INVESTIGATING AND COUNSELLING

Investigating and counselling refers to a strategy of dealing with an incident of pupil misbehaviour in an unthreatening, open-minded manner that – to some extent – does not explicitly acknowledge that misbehaviour has occurred (Kyriacou, 1998; McGuiness, 1993; Porter, 2000). If we notice a pupil prodding another pupil in the back with a pencil, or showing another pupil a magazine, or writing a message on a piece of paper, we can simply go over to that pupil and ask whether there is a problem, 'How are you getting on with the work?', or 'Do you know what you should be doing?' As soon as we have redirected the pupil back on task, we can then move away, although in some cases it is important to say that we will be checking all is well again in a few minutes' time, to help ensure they stay on task. This strategy is particularly useful in getting pupils back on task with the minimum of fuss, without having to be seen to have engaged in a conflict or made an issue out of the misbehaviour.

This approach can be extended into 'counselling'. Here, if the pupil has not responded well to the initial investigating stance, and we are having to return to the pupil in order to deal with the same misbehaviour, instead of resorting to reprimanding, we extend the investigating mode by talking more about the nature of the problem, asking ourselves: Why is the misbehaviour still occurring? Can we get the pupil to now agree more overtly that misbehaviour has occurred and needs to stop? It is essential here that the pupil agrees to this. If the 'counselling mode' is going to take more than a few minutes, it is better done in private at the end of the lesson. As such, we will have to ask the pupil to remain behind at the end of the lesson for a few minutes, or on occasions to come back and see us during a break period. This is not a reprimand or a punishment, however, rather it is simply an opportunity to extend the investigating mode, and to 'counsel' the pupil to understand that misbehaving is not in their best interests and that continued misbehaviour will create problems for us, them and for other pupils. It is essential that they verbally accept this and agree to co-operate in future. In this approach, we need to convey that we are on their side, supporting them and working in their best interests, and that if they misbehave again we can then convey we are disappointed and that they are letting themselves and us down.

The following qualities will increase the effectiveness when we use investigating and counselling approaches:

▶ *Establishing trust.* The conversation should take place in a context of trust, rapport and mutual respect.

▶ *Privacy.* It should take place in private (within the normative understandings of ethical probity).

▶ *Care.* The teacher should display a caring and concerned attitude towards the pupil, rather than a threatening, blaming and intimidating approach.

▶ *Encouraging reflection.* The pupil should be encouraged to evaluate his or her misbehaviour and the undesirable consequences which may follow if such misbehaviour continues, including a lack of educational progress, punishments or sanctions. It is important here for the pupil to do most of the talking not the teacher.

▶ *Achieving a positive resolution.* The pupil should be supported towards an agreement to behave in a more desirable way in the future, and accept that doing so is in their own best interests.

REPRIMANDING

Reprimanding refers to issuing a clear verbal statement of displeasure on our part concerning misbehaviour. It most commonly takes the form of telling a pupil what they have been doing or should be doing in an annoyed tone of voice: this does not mean we merely shout out 'Get on with your work!'; 'Stop that!'; 'You must put your hand up and not simply call out your answer'. Reprimands are more effective and less likely to cause disaffection when issued privately rather than shouted across the room, so that pupils do not react to public humiliation. It is better to reprimand the misbehaviour (e.g. not working) rather than the person (e.g. accusing the pupil of being lazy) so that we can show that we still feel positively about the pupil as a person, but it is the piece of misbehaviour we do not care for (Canter and Canter, 1992; Kyriacou, 1997; McManus, 1995).

Reprimands have an important role to play in maintaining discipline because they are easy to use, whereas investigating and counselling can be very time consuming. However, frequent use of reprimands can create a nagging tone to the lesson which can start to erode the maintenance of mutual respect and rapport.

The following points will increase the effectiveness of reprimands:

▶ *Target the correct pupil.* The pupil being reprimanded should be correctly identified as the pupil instigating or engaged in the misbehaviour. A particular danger here is to reprimand a pupil who was reacting to another's provocation.

▶ *Be firm.* Your reprimand should be clear and firm in tone and content. Avoid pleading or implying damage limitation (e.g. 'Let's at least get some decent work done in the last ten minutes') or softening your reprimand once issued.

▶ *Express concern.* Your reprimand should convey concern with the pupil's interests or that of the other pupils being affected or harmed by the misbehaviour.

▶ *Avoid inappropriate anger.* While a firm expression of disapproval is effective, expressing intense anger (shouting at pupils, appearing to have lost your temper) will tend to undermine a positive classroom climate. Frequent expressions of anger are undesirable, are experienced by pupils as unpleasant and, with younger pupils in particular, may be very upsetting.

▶ *Emphasise what is required.* Reprimands should emphasise what pupils *should* be doing rather than simply complain about the misbehaviour itself. 'Pay attention' is better than 'Stop looking out of the window', and 'You may talk quietly with your neighbour' is better than 'There's too much noise in here'.

▶ *Maintain psychological impact.* When a reprimand is given, its impact is enhanced by non-verbal cues, such as firm (non-threatening) eye contact. After the reprimand is given, a momentary prolonging of eye contact – together with a slight pause before continuing with the lesson – can increase the force of the exchange.

▶ *Avoid unnecessary confrontations.* It is very important we do not force a pupil into a heated exchange. Where such a possibility seems likely because the pupil seem tense, agitated or unresponsive to our pre-emptive strategies, postponing a reprimand and (instead) using investigating and counselling strategies would be more appropriate. If we reprimand a pupil who then reacts emotionally, we then usefully curtail the exchange by telling the pupil to stay behind at the end of the lesson in a matter of fact manner and quickly resume the lesson.

▶ *Focus on the behaviour not the pupil.* It is important to emphasize that we disapprove of the misbehaviour not the pupil. This enables us to convey a sense of caring for the pupil and their interests, and gives pupils an opportunity to dissociate themselves for such misbehaviour in future. 'You need to concentrate more on your work and spend less time chatting to others' is better than 'You're an idle person'.

▶ *Use private rather than public reprimands.* A private reprimand, such as a quiet word, is useful because it is a more personal contact and lessens the likelihood of embarrassing the pupil and reduces the likelihood that the pupil might react with hostility. It is also less disruptive for other pupils. A public reprimand to a pupil is appropriate, and necessary, only when there is a specific reason to 'go public', such as when we actually want the whole class to hear the reprimand as an implicit warning to others. A less disruptive use of a public reprimand is simply to call out the pupil's name in a tone that conveys that we noticed some misbehaviour which must stop immediately.

▶ *Act pre-emptively.* Reprimands aimed at pre-empting misbehaviour are more effective than those which follow only after repeated and prolonged misbehaviour.

▶ *State rules and rationale.* A reprimand can usefully consist of a statement of the rule being transgressed together with an explanation of why the rule is required for the benefit of teaching and learning (e.g. '[student's name] please put your hand up and wait until I ask you to speak so that everyone gets a fair chance to contribute and we can all hear what is said').

▶ *Avoid making hostile remarks.* Hostile and deprecating remarks should be avoided, as pupils may feel personally disliked, and may become disaffected and alienated. Sarcasm and ridicule in particular are felt by pupils to be unfair, and can undermine mutual respect and rapport to the detriment of a positive classroom climate.

▶ *Avoid unfair comparisons.* Pupils tend to feel reprimands which involve stereotyping or comparisons with others are unfair, particularly if they relate to other members of the pupil's family or other classes (e.g. 'Your sister's work is much better than this' or 'Just because this is set three doesn't mean you don't have to pay attention').

▶ *Seek to be consistent.* Reprimands should relate to clear and consistently applied expectations. Pupils will resent being reprimanded if they feel the behaviour was not the type we would normally reprimand or if the severity of the reprimand was unexpectedly great.

▶ *Do not make empty threats.* It is pointless issuing reprimands we would not wish to (or could not) carry out (e.g. 'The next pupil who talks will go straight to the head' or 'If you make another insolent remark, I shall be contacting your parents'). If we explicitly state the consequences that will follow, it is very important to carry these out if we are to maintain credibility when we use this strategy in the future.

▶ *Avoid reprimanding the whole class.* Reprimanding the whole class is a serious act and should only be used when certain misbehaviour or our cause for concern is so widespread that individual reprimands will not have sufficient effect or be appropriate. In order to avoid casting our criticism equally on all pupils (including the blameless) it is useful to indicate our concern with 'too many pupils' rather than all pupils. A useful alternative is to discuss with the class as a whole why certain misbehaviour has become widespread, so that we can identify any particular problems and reinforce the need for responsible behaviour.

▶ *'Make an example'.* Another useful alternative to reprimanding the whole class is to issue a particularly forceful reprimand to one pupil, and add or imply that you will not tolerate other pupils acting in this way. Reprimanding an individual can have just as much impact on the behaviour of the class as reprimanding the whole class. 'Making an example' can be particularly useful in the first few lessons with a new class to highlight our expectations, such as how we deal with the first pupil who arrives late for our lessons without any excuse. It is also useful if certain pupils appear to be trying to challenge our authority publicly; however, we must be sensitive concerning whether we are simply being drawn into a public confrontation that is best dealt with in some other way (i.e.: acknowledge lateness, welcome student, direct to a seat and follow up lateness issue later – away from the audience).

A judicious use of both 'investigating and counselling' on the one hand and 'reprimanding' on the other hand should be effective in dealing with distracting and disruptive misbehaviour that does occur from time to time in classes.

PUNISHMENTS

Beginning teachers sometimes take the view that if all else fails, there are punishments. Punishments can easily be seen as the heavy artillery that can come into play when the teacher is in trouble and that this sorts out the problem. In fact, punishments are not nearly as effective as new teachers would hope or expect. Most pupils who cannot be encouraged to behave through skilful use of the other strategies we have considered are unlikely to be transformed by punishments. Moreover, punishments can easily lead to resentment and disaffection. Punishment needs to be carried out with tremendous care (Barnes, 1999; Kyriacou, 1998; Munn *et al*, 1992).

Firstly, punishment should be use sparingly and as a last resort. Much discipline is maintained on the basis of convincing pupils that there is 'something worse down the line' that can be brought into play if misbehaviour persists. However, once they find out what that 'something' is, it may quickly lose its impact. Secondly, punishment must be used in a formal context. The message must be that the teacher is resorting to using a punishment because other avenues have failed, in the hope that a punishment might make the pupil realise the gravity of the situation they are facing. Punishment provides the pupil with an opportunity to stop, think and change course. If not, then it may be necessary to call in parents and other agencies, and the pupil's school career may be endangered with the threat of exclusion. In view of this, when we use punishment, we need to 'milk it for all it is worth'. We need to sermonise about it, we need to convey that it is being issued with a heavy heart and a deep concern for the pupil's future, and we need to make clear that it is being issued solely in the pupil's interests, not to make us or anyone else feel better. The purpose of punishment must be first and foremost educational, and only at a secondary level used for deterrence.

The points already considered that increase the effectiveness of reprimands also apply to the use of punishments. However, the following additional points are worthy of particular note:

► *Use sparingly.* Punishments should only be used sparingly and judiciously, and in the vast majority of cases only after other strategies have been tried.

► *Timing.* Punishments should be given as soon as possible after the misbehaviour. If there is a long delay, the link should be re-established at the time given.

► *Tone.* A punishment should be conveyed as an expression of our just and severe disapproval of the pupil's misbehaviour, and employed in the interests of the pupil and of the class as a whole. Punishment should not result from our losing our temper or appearing vindictive.

► *Punishment should be as related to the behaviour as possible.* The type and severity of the punishment should be appropriate to the misbehaviour but should also take account of the context.

► *Due process.* It is important that the pupil accepts that the punishment is fair and just. This will normally mean that the pupil has been warned that such a consequence may follow, and that our expectations and actions regarding such misbehaviour are clear and consistent. The pupil should also be asked to explain the misbehaviour and encouraged to understand and accept why the punishment is just, deserved and appropriate.

▶ *Relating to school policy.* The punishment should relate to the overall policy of the school towards discipline.

▶ *'Aversiveness'.* Some pupils may not mind being sent out of the room, or may even gain status in the eyes of peers as a result. Therefore, each punishment needs to be of a type that is 'aversive' for the pupil concerned and minimises any factors that are likely to affect or weaken its effectiveness, bearing in mind the need to be fair and consistent.

DIFFICULT PUPILS AND DIFFICULT CLASSES

The vast majority of pupils will behave well most of the time, and their misbehaviour can be dealt with using strategies that involve a minimum of fuss and effort. However, some teachers will face difficult pupils in difficult schools where the behaviour is particularly challenging and where the more usual strategies only appear to have a limited effect. Much has been written about the additional strategies that skilful teachers can use in such circumstances that can be helpful (Blum, 1998; Cowley, 2001; Rogers, 1997). Unfortunately, there are no simple or easy solutions in these circumstances. Difficult pupils have often experienced problems outside the school and/or have experienced problems in school with their own learning that has resulted in them being very suspicious of teachers and learning. In such circumstances it is easy to advocate the need to be firmer, harsher and to make more frequent use of punishment. However, success in this case seems to depend much more on the skilful use of setting short-term and achievable goals for such pupils coupled with a generous use of encouragement in order gradually to nurture them into a feeling that learning can become a safe and rewarding experience. What is also true, however, is that such pupils are capable of taking advantage of any laxness on the part of the teacher. A one-hour lesson may go immensely well for the first forty-five minutes, only for us to ease up in our vigilance as the end approaches, allowing some idle chat to develop further, and before you know it a heated argument with fists flying has developed out of nothing. When teaching such pupils, continued firmness and vigilance are crucial. In such circumstances, approaches to behaviour management in which systematic use of praise for good behaviour is coupled with clear directions from the teacher about the behaviour that is required can be very effective in establishing and maintaining good discipline, particularly if this approach is also linked to a consistent whole-school policy on discipline (Clarke and Murray, 1996; Gillborn *et al*, 1992; Rogers, 1995).

A HUMANISTIC VIEW OF DISCIPLINE

The increasing awareness of the importance of fostering pupils' self-esteem has been a major development in discipline over the years. This view has a long pedigree and stems in part from its emphasis within humanistic psychology and its applications to education, notably through the work of Abraham Maslow and Carl Rogers (e.g. Maslow, 1987; Rogers and Freiberg, 1994). They both argued that education must place an emphasis on the whole person, on the idea of personal growth, on the pupil's own perspective in terms of how they see themselves and see the world, and on the notions of personal agency and the power of choice. The key elements in applying this humanistic approach to classroom teaching involve:

(i)   Seeing the teacher's role as essentially that of being a facilitator.
(ii) Providing a significant degree of choice and control to pupils to manage and organise their learning.
(iii) Displaying respect for and empathy with pupils.

A humanistic approach to discipline would thus involve an emphasis on providing a learning environment in which the pupil felt confident and empowered to learn, and where the pupil would be helped and encouraged to see classroom discipline as a matter stemming from the self-discipline of each pupil. The ethos of the classroom would be supportive in tone and the teacher would convey warmth and a caring disposition towards all pupils. Indeed, Rogers, in particular, argued that one of the hallmarks of the humanistic teacher was their ability to maintain an 'unconditional positive regard' towards all pupils.

These ideals, of course, are often hard to sustain in practice. For example, a study by Kyriacou and Cheng (1993) asked 109 student teachers at the beginning of their teacher training course to rate the strength of their agreement with 20 statements regarding the humanistic approach to teaching and learning. A sample of the student teachers were interviewed later in the year after they had completed a block of teaching practice in schools. The study reported that the vast majority of the student teachers agreed with the humanistic approach, but those interviewed after their teaching practice said they had found it hard to put these qualities into practice. For example, they found it difficult to maintain a positive regard towards all their pupils and also to allow pupils a marked degree of control over their learning activities. These findings accord with other studies indicating that most teachers hold such humanistic views as 'ideals' but feel that the constraints and realities of classroom life and pupils' attitudes often make it difficult to sustain these in practice. Despite these difficulties, the classroom climate in schools has become much more 'humanistic' (and certainly more 'humane') in its tone over the years.

The need to foster pupils' self-esteem as learners is fundamental to the humanistic approach, and the most important influence on pupils' self-esteem in the classroom is our interaction with them. If our comments to pupils are largely positive, supportive, encouraging, praising, valuing and relaxing, rather than negative, deprecating, harsh, attacking, dominating and anxiety-provoking, this will do much to foster pupils' self-esteem.

In addition, our body language also communicates to pupils how we feel about them, through messages conveyed non-verbally by our use of eye contact, posture and facial expression. It can be difficult to convey a message verbally about how we feel if our body language indicates to pupils something different. An awareness of how what we say and our body language is likely to be perceived by pupils can help us to develop the skills necessary to establish a positive classroom climate. Nevertheless, positive messages are much easier to convey if our feelings are consistent with what we are seeking to convey: viz we genuinely do like and respect pupils, care for their learning and feel relaxed and confident in our role as teacher.

Another important feature of the humanistic approach to discipline would be reflected in the emphasis placed on discussing with pupils the need to adopt certain rules to enable order in the classroom to be maintained. The teacher would discuss with pupils what rules were needed and why, and these would then be agreed rather than unilaterally imposed by the teacher. These rules would be reviewed from time to time to check they were working well and whether the rules needed to be changed.

Humanistic teachers would also tend to use 'investigating and counselling' as the primary means of dealing with any pupil misbehaviour that arises, and this would be linked to reminding the pupil of their need for self-discipline and encouraging them.

CONCLUSIONS

As a result of the wealth of writings and research findings on discipline we now have a good understanding of the general qualities involved in effective behaviour management that will help teachers establish and maintain discipline in the classroom. Nevertheless, doing this in practice involves a high level of skill and expertise on the part of teachers, and even the best teachers will encounter circumstances where things go wrong. That is to a large extent inevitable given the complex nature of human behaviour, and the element of unpredictability in how pupils will respond to a particular strategy in a particular context.

The central message of this chapter is that teachers must not think that discipline is achieved through an authoritarian approach in their dealings with pupils. Rather, discipline needs to be based on establishing a classroom climate where there is mutual respect and rapport; acceptance by pupils of the teacher's authority; good teaching; and skilful use by the teacher of low-level, non-intrusive strategies that quickly deal with emerging misbehaviour and get pupils back on task with the minimum fuss and disruption to the lesson.

When I first came across the adage 'Don't smile until Christmas', I took this to be simply a warning to new teachers that becoming over-friendly towards pupils can undermine the establishment of one's authority. Whilst I agree that in the first few lessons with a new class it is important to establish a businesslike purposefulness to the teaching, and to display authority with an appropriate display of assertiveness and firmness, the adage has, perhaps, encouraged too many new teachers to neglect the importance of building a positive relationship with pupils based on mutual respect and rapport. Showing humanity, and humour from time to time, is crucial to a teacher's role. I would want to say, yes, we can smile from time to time. Indeed, we need to smile (!). Yes, we can show that we enjoy being in the company of pupils. And, yes, we can take a humanistic view of discipline.

REFERENCES

Barnes, R. (1999) *Positive Teaching, Positive Learning.* London: Routledge.

Blum, P. (1998) *Surviving and Succeeding in Difficult Classrooms.* London: Routledge.

Canter, L. and Canter, M. (1992) *Assertive Discipline.* Santa Monica, California: Lee Canter and Associates.

Clarke, D. and Murray, A. (eds.) (1996) *Developing and Implementing a Whole-School Behaviour Policy : A Practical Approach.* London: David Fulton.

Cooper, P. and McIntyre, D. (1996) *Effective Teaching and Learning: Teachers' and Students' Perspectives.* Buckingham: Open University Press.

Cowley, S. (2001) *Getting the Buggers to Behave.* London: Continuum.

Dean, J. (1996) *Beginning Teaching in the Secondary School.* Buckingham: Open University Press.

Gillborn, D., Nixon, J. and Ruddock, J. (1992) *Dimensions of Discipline: Rethinking Practice in Secondary Schools.* London: HMSO.

Kyriacou, C. (1997) *Effective Teaching in Schools* (2nd edn.). Cheltenham: Nelson Thornes.

Kyriacou, C. (1998) *Essential Teaching Skills* (2nd edn.). Cheltenham: Nelson Thornes.

Kyriacou, C. and Cheng, H. (1993) Student teachers' attitudes towards the humanistic approach to learning and learning in schools. *European Journal of Teacher Education,* vol. 16, pp 163–168.

Maslow, A. H. (1987) *Motivation and Personality* (3rd edn.). New York: Harper Collins.

McGuinness, J. (1993) *Teachers, Pupils and Behaviour: A Managerial Approach.* London: Cassell.

McManus, M. (1995) *Troublesome Children in the Classroom: Meeting Individual Needs* (2nd edn.). London: Routledge.

Morgan, C. and Morris, G. (1999) *Good Teaching and Learning: Pupils and Teachers Speak.* Buckingham: Open University Press.

Munn, P., Johnstone, M. and Chambers, V. (1992) *Effective Discipline in Secondary Schools and Classrooms.* London: Swift.

Pollard, A., Triggs, P., Broadfoot, P., McNess, E. and Osborn, M. (2000) *What Pupils Say: Changing Policy and Practice in Primary Education.* London: Continuum.

Porter, L. (2000) *Behaviour in Schools: Theory and Practice for Teachers.* Buckingham: Open University Press.

Robertson, J. (1996) *Effective Classroom Control* (3rd edn.). London: Hodder & Stoughton.

Rogers, B. (1997) *Cracking the Hard Class.* London: Paul Chapman.

Rogers, B. (1995) *Behaviour Management: A Whole School Approach.* London: Paul Chapman.

Rogers, C. R. and Freiberg, H. J. (1994) *Freedom to Learn* (3rd edn.). New York: Merrill.

4

The Balance Model: minimalism in behaviour management

Christine Richmond

Managing human behaviour, particularly children's behaviour, is a perpetual challenge. It can seem, at times, complex and demanding. When children's behaviour is attentionally challenging management is also quite stressful. In this essay, Christine Richmond explores the essential teacher-student communication present in management and discipline contexts. Christine develops a 'model of balance' exploring how the language of expectation, acknowledgement and correction affect learning and behaviour. Christine's research in behaviour management indicates that there is often a skew, in teacher's management and discipline, to a language of correction.

Within her model Christine explores the core skills and strategies that can bring balance to necessary correction, acknowledgement, affirmation, encouragement and support.

This chapter unapologetically contains simple ways of understanding behaviour management and disruptive student behaviour. De Bono (1998) discusses the relevance of developing simple processes to help people negotiate the complexities of contemporary life. Managing the behaviour of students in today's inclusive classes is an extremely complex business. Teaching is so intensely demanding that 'cutting to the chase', as demonstrated by the simple models in this chapter, are designed to help teachers move quickly into an easier and more relaxed way of managing. A minimalist approach to behaviour management practice introduced here is intended to help teachers learn to pour the bulk of their energy and enthusiasm into curriculum conversations with students.

I hypothesise that the interactions teachers have in the classroom can be sorted into two main types: curriculum-focused language and management-focused language. Curriculum-focused language incorporates all teaching interactions aimed at eliciting or imparting curriculum-based information. Management-focused language is a higher-level communication process undertaken by teachers to prompt students to access the curriculum successfully though co-operative behaviour. It incorporates three separate but related sets of language, the languages of expectation, acknowledgment and correction.

DEFINITIONS

The language of expectation incorporates what teachers say and do to **articulate the boundaries** of acceptable social and working behaviour in the classroom. The language of acknowledgment incorporates what teachers say and do to **encourage and support** students in their endeavours to engage with the curriculum and to behave co-operatively with others. The language of correction incorporates what teachers say and do to **interrupt and refocus** students who are off-task and disrupting others. The key to effective, minimalist management occurs when these operate together in what I call the Balance Model (see Figure 1). When teachers articulate clear boundaries and provide balanced feedback in the form of supportive encouragement together with timely, respectful correction for the class as a whole and students individually they achieve a balance in behaviour management language.

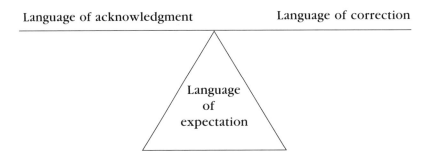

Figure 1. The Balance Model

The Balance Model is an original construct that underpins contemporary management theories. It can be thought of as a meta-construct that is generic to these models. Many theorists such as Porter (2000) usefully discuss the *differences* between theories of behaviour, whereas the Balance Model is a description of what is the same to them.

My research into the management styles of some teachers reveals that they tend to skew the management-focused communications towards correction with insufficient attention to the language of expectation and little to acknowledgment. It may be that teachers regard correction as synonymous with behaviour management rather than being a sub-set of it.

In my experience, teachers tend to skew their management towards correction when under pressure to manage those with particularly challenging behaviours. When a balance between the amount and quality of correcting and acknowledging feedback is not achieved (see Figure 2), students who are fragile, such as those with behavioural challenges and long-term learning difficulties move into a recursive relationship of teacher correction and student disruption that is difficult to interrupt. The teacher's relationship with such students

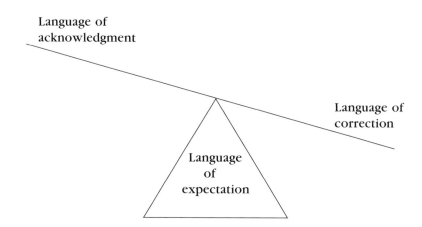

Figure 2. Skew of traditional behaviour management

becomes fraught as this cycle of corrective interaction is maintained over time and the relationship progressively deteriorates.

Additionally when working with students with particularly challenging behaviours teachers appear to want evidence of generous amounts of co-operative behaviour before giving acknowledging feedback. Unfortunately, three problems prevent students responding to correction and changing their behaviour in this way:

1   The student with challenging behaviours typically has a history of school failure. He or she has a 'failure habit'. In order to cope with this painful and self-defeating experience, the student logically develops, practises and refines a range of defensive, self-protective behaviours that can include acting out and avoiding contact with the curriculum.

2   Sometimes teachers, who are under intense pressure to be accountable and do the myriad tasks that are clustered under their ever-expanding role, can fail to notice incremental positive changes that a student with challenging behaviours might make.

3   It is commonplace for teachers to comment that they resent paying positive attention to a student who occasionally does what others students nearly always do.

This 'faultless common sense' helps maintain an uncomfortable status quo in the classroom. It is within the teacher's reach, however, to make a positive difference to this equation but it takes intentional effort in a planned rather than ad hoc way. Unfortunately, teachers are not necessarily thoroughly prepared in the higher-level communication behaviour management skills required by their work. Other professionals such as lawyers and counsellors are trained in the higher-level communication skills they need, but teachers have often been left largely to their own devices in this matter.

How do teachers come to grips with this aspect of their work? Initially they have to accept that the communication aspect of behaviour management is learnable, that it does not 'come naturally' as those who are gifted communicators may make it appear. Also, expert teachers who have thoroughly internalised good behaviour management practice may well have forgotten how they acquired their own skills. This is a well documented characteristic of experts in other fields such as nursing (Benner, 1994).

Secondly, teachers must collectively transcend the tendency towards traditional, over-correcting styles of managing others in order to reach a more balanced and supportive style. With this in mind the following metaphors and models may be useful.

WHAT IS BEHAVIOUR MANAGEMENT?

Behaviour management is like housework. Some people do it as they go, just as they clean tiles when they take a shower. Others use a blitz approach, doing it every now and then with little in between. Then there are those who resent having to do it, blame students for not wanting to learn, and expect others (parents, school administrators) to make order out of the chaos they have inevitably helped to create through lack of action. As much as we might resent doing it (as we commonly dislike doing housework), we cannot avoid managing the behaviour of students without counterproductive consequences. Like housework, behaviour management is a relentless cycle of activity with its own ebbs and flows and schedules. Management is also fraught with complex issues outside of schools that negatively affect the behaviour of some of our students.

DISRUPTIVE BEHAVIOUR

It is important to accept the heterogeneous nature of the student population. Without considering variability in learning styles, academic ability, schooling history, family background, or something as pervasive as social values; even sociability itself might also be distributed according to a normal curve (see Figure 3). Students with stable, fragile internal controls (or poor self-control) are less likely – for example – to co-operate in class, put litter in the bin even when somebody is watching, or complete assignments on time. These students are likely to present as management challenges for the duration of their schooling across different settings. They are particularly 'expensive' to teach on all measures, including time, energy, and resources.

Most students represented by the middle of the curve, however, behave differently in different settings in response to complex sets of internal and

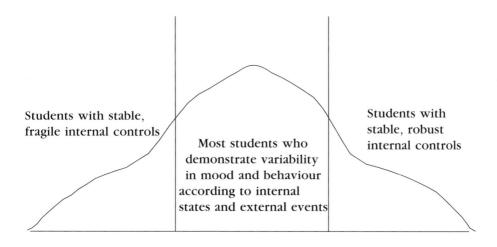

Students with stable, fragile internal controls

Most students who demonstrate variability in mood and behaviour according to internal states and external events

Students with stable, robust internal controls

Figure 3. Hypothetical heterogeneity in the sociability of student population

external influences. For example, people express wide variability in such highly personal features as locus of control and levels of stress (Kyriacou and Sutcliffe, 1979). External variables such as time of day, curriculum area and teaching styles also influence student behaviour. Being on playground duty on a windy, rainy day reveals how much the weather influences many students' behaviour.

Finally, there is a small group of students with stable, robust internal controls. These are more likely to, for example, always co-operate in class; put litter in the bin (even when nobody is watching) and complete assignments on time. These students are independent learners and tend to be academically successful. They rarely present as management challenges and are relatively 'inexpensive' to teach (in the sense noted earlier). It is not surprising that some schools in the private sector tend to openly vie for such students through scholarship mechanisms, and discourage those with fragile internal controls through enrolment strictures, in order to maximise student outcomes.

In addition to the management implications brought by heterogeneity in the student population (skewed in state schools towards the left in the model above, and in private schools to the right), student disruption is also affected by the coercive nature of schooling itself. Coercion almost unfailingly invites resistance of one type or another in some schools. If people are required to be in a certain space for a mandated length of time, work beside people with whom they don't necessarily want to associate and participate in activities they have not chosen, it is not surprising that disruptive behaviours occur.

The 'coercion factor' becomes increasingly salient as students become more sophisticated and independent in their teens. Secondary teachers, in particular, need to have a robust repertoire of behaviour management skills as they address adolescent behaviour in schools. Some of these self teachers, however excellent they may be as exponents of their curriculum specialities, tend to skew management toward suppressing disruption in the best ways that they know how when students rebel against a learning environment that is sometimes seriously out of touch with contemporary mores of interpersonal communication. This could be an outcome of our collective post-colonial heritage (in Australia) where some of those with power have ridden roughshod over those in their charge.

Reflecting on our colonial past, community conversations inevitably include notions that the decision-making regarding power and coercion at the time was well intentioned. Thankfully in the 21st century we are increasingly coming to understand the oppressive behaviour of that time as seriously flawed. I believe traditional behaviour management practices that linger uncontested in some schools have to change in order for teachers and students to relax and enjoy the schooling process. Behaviour management will change of course, but at what cost? Ex-pupils are beginning to litigate for compensation for the rough treatment meted out to them at school. Both human and economic costs associated with losing disenfranchised students from the system through academic failure, together with a cycle of persistent punishment for disobedience, are too great to maintain.

A model of resistance presented below seeks to illustrate that no matter how exciting the curriculum, how engaging the teaching process, some students will present what could be called a psychologically logical response (in regard to their private logic) when put under pressure to conform. Understanding this has the potential to liberate teachers from taking student disruption personally. Taking student behaviour as a personal affront is one of those insidious factors that has the power to increase stress and undermine effective communication. Many teachers resolve this personalisation factor as they gain experience, however it is not always the case. Some teachers maintain anguish, and some even a self-righteous student-blaming stance, well into their veteran years. These teachers often work well with co-operative students but have great difficulty successfully helping students with fragile internal controls access the curriculum. Seeing disruption as a professionally challenging issue that is not tinged with personal malice takes a lot of professional self-reflection and practice. However, regarding some disruptive behaviour as *malicious* encourages unnecessary angst in the short term, and has the potential to build – over time – into long-term stress, and thereby contribute to teachers' dissatisfaction with work. It actively prevents these teachers developing robust, respectful and professional relationships with all students. It also prevents them from enjoying their life's work. As Byrne (1994, 665) notes:

> As the social climate of the classroom deteriorates, teachers become emotionally exhausted and develop increasingly negative attitudes towards their students and the teaching profession.

The resistance model provides an alternative way to conceptualise much off-task behaviour. It contains four types of behaviour within a matrix formed by two axes: these are pro-social and anti-social, and covert and overt. Pro-social, covert behaviour is the apparently polite behaviour of some students who nevertheless fail to engage in curriculum learning at a meaningful (for them) level. These students tend to attract little teacher attention compared with those who disrupt, because they appear obedient. Anti-social, covert behaviour is characterised by students who continue to amuse themselves with their own activities despite teachers' efforts to gain their attention to task.

There are two sub-types of overt, pro-social resistance. One type is the assertive 'I don't want to do this because it has no relevance to my life' thematic comment of some students' courageous protestations. The other is characterised by students who pretend to work whenever the teacher is vigilant but then resume off-task, yet not disruptive, behaviour, when the teacher moves away. Anti-social, overt behaviour spans a continuum with mild, usually high frequency disruptive behaviours at one end and severe, usually (and thankfully) low frequency disruptive behaviours at the other. Disruptive behaviours at the mild end might include interrupting, arriving late, or calling out across the classroom. Disruptive behaviours at the other end might include threatening behaviour, temper tantrums or physical aggression.

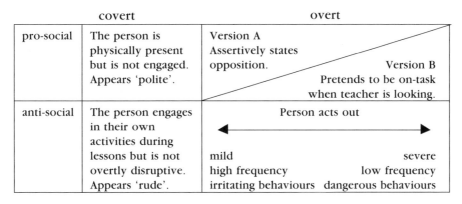

Figure 4. Resistance to coercion

I argue that resistance is a logical human response to coercion. For example, most people behave politely when they make social duty visits to relatives with whom they feel they must maintain a relationship despite the fact that they don't enjoy the contact (pro-social, covert). Political activists stand up for human rights in repressive regimes despite the social cost (pro-social, overt, version A). Many people in these repressive regimes superficially adhere to laws and are overtly loyal to the state but collude with like-minded people who covertly oppose its strictures when they can do so with relative safety (pro-social, overt, version B). People with poor self-control behave in ways that span the mild to severe continuum (anti-social, overt) when they perceive their wants and needs to be thwarted. Correction facilities are full of people who have low frustration tolerance thresholds such as this. Correction facilities are also full of desperate, helpless and hopeless people who have had fractured educational opportunities and who come from poverty stricken backgrounds. These people get caught in lifestyles that are 'expensive' to run. The groups I have described are not mutually exclusive. I also must mention the unlucky souls who get caught doing what many other people in the community do without apparent penalty.

By contemplating the ramifications of resistance (described in the model), teachers can liberate themselves from the burden of **being responsible for their students' behaviour** and use that energy to invest in taking **full responsibility for managing** student behaviour as efficiently as possible. This epistemological flip appears subtle; it isn't. The beliefs teachers hold directly impact not only on the style of behaviour management they are likely to adopt, but also on their attitudes about their work, and therefore, on moment-by-moment classroom decision making.

Management, however clever, cannot be effective unless it goes hand in hand with a relevant, engaging curriculum taught with enthusiasm and a sprinkling, at least, of joy. If teachers are boring, uninspiring, unprepared or do not like being with young people, they should be supportively supervised to 'lift their game'. The overwhelming majority of teachers however are dedicated and full of concern about the enormity of the work of teaching.

The Balance Model introduced at the beginning of the chapter is a simple way to identify key language and activity sets that are necessary for efficiently developing respectful relationships with learners.

MINIMALIST SKILLS IN THE BALANCE MODEL

The Balance Model, as mentioned previously, comprises the teacher using three management-focused languages in concert. These are the languages of expectation, acknowledgment and correction. The **language of expectation** comprises what teachers say and do to communicate socially appropriate boundaries. Minimalist skills in this area include rule making and instruction giving. While there are well-established guidelines for making useful rules in the behaviour management literature, a teacher could easily be overwhelmed by the complexity of the recommended best practice. Minimalism in this area is imposing a few, positively stated and visually available rules. Some will be horrified by my suggested lack of collaboration with students about this important issue; however, I make three practical points learned from hard experience. Firstly, in a secondary school, if every teacher discussed and designed rules with students, the first week of each term would be devoted to extremely tedious and repetitive discussions from the point of view of the learner. Secondly, some classes are so chaotic, especially at the beginning of term, that it is difficult for new teachers in particular to facilitate useful discussions. Thirdly, teachers are paid to take responsibility for communicating their expectations. The time for negotiation is probably *after* students have learned about the boundaries the teacher is accountable to maintain.

Another key skill in the language of expectation is **giving effective instructions** to help students negotiate transitions successfully. Transitions are those times when students are moving in and out of rooms, from group to group in the classroom, and beginning and finishing activities. Students with less well-developed self-control frequently find it difficult to contain themselves during these times and take the opportunity to disrupt. This actively interferes with the 'smooth flow of lessons' that Kounin (1970) originally described as a key factor in teaching well.

Effective instructions are cued, start with a verb, are said once in an assertive voice and are followed by a period of waiting and scanning for compliance. Instructions are difficult for some teachers who believe that using a commanding tone of voice is impolite. These teachers prefer to make requests. Unfortunately, requests communicate that compliance is optional.

The **language of acknowledgment** comprises what teachers say and do to support on-task and socially co-operative behaviour. There are three fundamental types of acknowledgment. These are: the teacher's body language, verbalisations about students' pro-social and on-task behaviour and the use of visual representations of performance. Teachers can use body language to encourage students to stay on-task by moving near those who are working and by appropriately touching the student's materials. Many teachers with whom I have worked have found that this strategy has two outcomes. Firstly, it cues them to move around their classes as they teach and, secondly, students appear to appreciate the minimal attention and stay on-task for longer periods. I receive overwhelmingly positive feedback about the effectiveness of this minimalist strategy across the year levels.

Another body language technique that teachers find facilitates co-operation is standing at the door and welcoming students with direct eye contact as they enter the classroom. In my experience teachers say they do this, but as I move around the schools I don't see much evidence to support this assertion. I learned the usefulness of this strategy when I helped bus drivers with the management of students during the dreaded after-school shift. Bus drivers typically have less communication flexibility than schoolteachers. While observing several drivers during this shift I noticed that they looked either out of the window or at the consul that distributed tickets. A few bus drivers trialled what I suggested and made eye contact with as many passengers as possible and reported there was a subsequent positive change in behaviour. I hypothesised that by changing the direction of the gaze, these bus drivers let passengers know they were recognised, and thereby decreased the invitation for them to disappear into an anonymous group. Unfortunately, most of the cohort of bus drivers did not want to take responsibility for increasing their influence by changing their own behaviour, preferring to remain stuck in a 'blame-the-passenger' framework. Some bus drivers were so frustrated they angrily recommended flogging – (hmmm!).

Another powerful body language technique is 'non-contingent smiling' (that is, smiling for no particular reason) at students who are particularly fragile. Many students with poor self-control believe that teachers do not like them (and they may very well be correct; such students are not easy to appreciate). It is useful to perturb this dangerous idea. It is not easy to learn if negative feelings dominate the relationship. Obviously it is impossible to keep smiling throughout the day, but increasing the amount of smiling is something everyone could practise without much effort or training. Sometimes this strategy elicits a 'What are you looking at?' response. By answering questions such as these the teacher risks buying into secondary behaviours (Rogers 1990). Alternatively, this response can be celebrated as evidence that the student has noticed a difference.

Verbal acknowledgment is much debated in the literature. For example, Balson (1994) believes that praise ruins students' motivation. Alternatively, my experience is that telling students about their on-task and socially co-operative behaviour as accurately and simply as possible informs development of an internal language of self-control. One of the ways we learn about ourselves is by what people say to us about us (see Vignette 1).

As a young child I had no idea I was intelligent until a primary school teacher told me. His words resonated deeply. The moment is deeply embedded in my psyche, and contests other moments when I was chastised and belittled. It is no surprise which moments build strength and provide language constructs for the development of esteem and self control, and which do not.

Vignette 1 Power of verbal acknowledgment

I advise teachers to be generous with their acknowledgment of students' learning attempts but to do so with sensitivity in order to avoid potential embarrassment. Sensitivity, in a practical sense, means that teachers should privately acknowledge individuals and save enthusiastic congratulations for the class group. I cringe with empathetic embarrassment when robust pubescent students are called out during school assembly for improved behaviour awards. This superficially positive practice may put the student 'at risk' in the playground; need I go on? It is important to reflect on the consequences of our expressions of goodwill and support. Some fragile students have told me that they are so terrified at being singled out for public approval by teachers that they do their best not to attract it. Minimal verbal acknowledgment is describing exactly what the student does that is on-task and co-operative in a matter-of-fact voice. Some teachers prefer to use 'warm fuzzies' such as 'good', 'wonderful' or 'terrific'. I believe that while these might convey approval they do not provide the student with the information they require to build a repertoire of self-knowledge. 'You started straight away', is a much more powerful acknowledgment and is much less likely to attract regurgitation finger signals as you turn to walk away!

Fragile learners do not always believe adults who recognise and describe their positive features, particularly when the reflected strength is contested by the students' poor self-regard. Many of these students have experienced some level of adult manipulation and retaliate against anything that looks and sounds like manipulation. In these cases I recommend the intermittent use of **visual displays of performance**. These displays are evidence of improvement over time and are particularly useful when students are in crisis (see Figure 5). In this figure the arrows indicate supportive intervention to help the student in crisis regain connection with the curriculum. Teachers commonly work with their peers, an administrator, school counsellor or behaviour support teacher to develop and implement suitable scaffolds (represented as arrows in Figure 5). The scaffolds can be as simple as a tick chart that allows the teacher or student to monitor co-operative or on-task behaviour or can be as complex as a token economy. I recommend beginning as simply as possible. The excelled applied behaviour analysis text by Alberto and Troutman (1995) contains a comprehensive guide to the development of more complex tracking devices.

Students with fragile internal controls commonly experience a series of crises. Unfortunately teachers sometimes have great difficulty implementing this type of strategy multiple times. I believe this is due to two factors. The first is a feeling of disappointment engendered in the first place by the hope that the student's problem could be 'fixed' by the first intervention. Behaviour management rarely, if ever, fixes behaviour problems; it just manages them. People learn new behaviours but rarely drop practiced ones out of their repertoire permanently (backsliding ex-smokers can attest to that). Even our most primitive childhood responses to trauma can re-emerge in adulthood when external conditions are problematic enough. All of us are a sum of our experiences; we are all of who we have ever been.

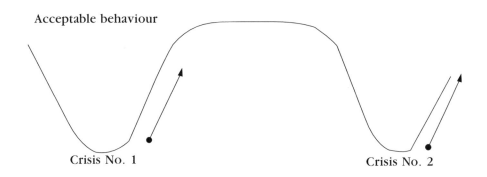

Figure 5. Intermittent crisis profile

Secondly, teachers tend to believe that their additional work during the original crisis was wasted and tend to express resentment about the 'wasted effort'. Again, this is not so, the student regained an approximation of stability and practised this for a time. The most teachers can expect from these students, who typically lead extraordinarily complex and challenging lives, is that crises might get less intense and erupt less frequently over time.

Sometimes teachers argue that they should not have to provide this kind of support when other students (and the focus student at times) co-operate successfully without it. However, there are two important issues that underpin the rationale for providing such support. The first point is contained in the distribution curve in Figure 3 that clearly demonstrates some students do not have sufficient self-control to manage themselves, particularly when they are under a great deal of stress. In my experience, students in this situation do not necessarily look unhappy; their demeanours might reflect a wide range of affect, from surliness to robust cheekiness. Children learn in early childhood how best to behave in order to keep threatening adults at bay. It becomes difficult to maintain the energy required to keep returning to 'scaffolding building' if teachers expect quick and sustained improvement in behaviour. We have to learn to be satisfied with incremental positive change interspersed with crises that emerge at intervals. An optimistic profile is where crises erupt less frequently and each is less traumatic.

The power of 'scaffolds' can be represented by the metaphor in Figure 6. The broken leg represents the student's disconnection from the curriculum. The cast is the scaffold created by him or her (if possible) in collaboration with teachers and others. Concern about the deleterious effects of extrinsic motivation is seen for what it is when we consider this metaphor. The cast – that is the visual representation of the performance – merely arrests counterproductive move-ment while internal processes heal the fracture. When a leg breaks a second time, doctors don't say, 'Well we used a cast last time but it didn't work.' Not all children break their legs so not all need casts. Casts don't stay on for a long time; as a matter of fact they are removed as soon as limbs show improvement and are replaced with firm bandages. Texts on applied behaviour analysis, such as Kaplan's (1995) *Beyond Behaviour Modification: A cognitive-behavioural approach to classroom management,* provide practical information about fading support to maximise the positive effects of these kinds of interventions.

Another issue underpinning the concern teachers express about support processes of this nature is the concept of social justice versus retributory justice. The socially just response to a crisis situation is one where students get what they *need* in order to reconnect as quickly as possible with the curriculum. The retributory process is one where students get what others judge they *deserve*. Frankly, a teacher can spend his or her entire professional life disseminating retributory justice to school students (and some deputy principals do); it doesn't work, it never has. It increases the likelihood that students will resent the schooling process and inexorably become further disenfranchised.

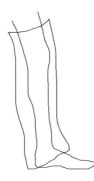

Figure 6. A metaphor for crisis intervention

Accept that these students, as unappealing to teach as they can be, and as irritatingly time- and energy-absorbing as they inevitably are, are nevertheless young learners who need repeated opportunities to discover that their teachers care. One powerful way of doing this is by repeatedly managing the students' crises as calmly and thoughtfully as possible. Teachers who problem-solve rather than punish – with the (thankfully) metaphorical stick – are on the social justice track. School systems gave up caning students because human rights legislation prohibits this kind of punishment. However, some remain committed to the idea that punishment has therapeutic value. All schools have not addressed a collective retributive mindset and some tend to remain oriented to dishing out overwhelming amounts of punitive consequences to students (see vignette 2). It doesn't work and it is not ethical in an education endeavour. It is particularly unethical in a state system where we aim to teach *all* students who misbehave.

> *Consider the plight of the non-academic youth whose greatest strength is weaving a magic spell on the football field. Some teachers might be attracted to the idea that if this student breaks the rules in class he should be deprived of joining the game. A socially just process recognises that the student's source of honour and pride, his football prowess, needs to be the foundation for strength building in other areas.*

Vignette 2 Correction as punishing rather than teaching

The **language of correction** is an area that is unnecessarily fraught with difficulties. I have already touched on some issues that contribute to this. The first and most fundamental point is that correction at school should be designed to interrupt disruptive behaviour and teach the student what to do to reconnect with the curriculum. Instead it is commonly articulated through punishment (as explored above) and sometimes wasted on behaviour that is irritating to the teacher but not necessarily disruptive.

Criminal behaviour such as violent, premeditated assault particularly with a weapon in students of responsible age should be handled with police support. Here I do not infer that police involvement is necessary in the case, for example, of a tantrum where scissors are thrown. This is a dangerous event but it is not a premeditated assault.

Suspension has a role for dangerous events. It signals to the community that something serious has happened, it gives the teachers a break from the student, and it alerts care givers about the discrepancy between school expectations and student performance. During the suspension it is useful for school personnel to get together to review the student's learning plan so that the administrator is up to date on the student's progress and prepared for the re-entry interview. However, the longer a student is away from school the harder he or she has to work to feel confident about coming back, and some students don't have the capacity to do this kind of work at all. They can enter the interview in a very fragile state and need a lot of emotional support to be able to do the work that is required from a more relaxed frame of mind. I believe the one-day, then three-day, then twenty-day suspension schedule commonly used in schools in some Australian states does not meet the educational needs of students who typically have learning difficulties associated with their behaviour problems. Alternatively, I recommend using suspensions that are as brief as possible and provide students with multiple opportunities to meet the teachers to problem solve. Connecting students to others who have managed their own difficult times is also helpful. Administrators could also use an expert team of previously suspended students to help them work out ways to make it less likely for students to experience this overt rejection.

The re-entry from suspension interview should focus on how the student can reconnect with the curriculum and regain the trust of the school community, in that order. The details of these conversations are ideally worked out in collaboration with the student and care giver. The ideal outcome is a practical, small plan that can be monitored by the student and a nominated teacher. If the interviewer is punitive, however, and scolds the student he or she is likely to decrease respect for the entire enterprise of schooling and is much more likely to revert to defensive, hostile behaviour. Everyone appreciates being treated with respect; since adults are being paid to work at school and students are not, it is relatively easy for adults to go the 'extra mile' when students cannot find it in themselves to demonstrate respect.

ABOUT CORRECTION

In a balanced behaviour management intervention, the correction is ideally short, and carried out in three or four consecutive steps. A decision to correct should be made sooner rather than later when disruptive behaviour emerges. It is crucial that the students who attract correction see and hear the teacher managing the situation from a calm perspective. It is almost immaterial what strategies are used as long as they are consistently and fairly applied and allow students enough space to maintain what self-respect they have. Public humiliation in any form is counterproductive to this endeavour. Intervening earlier makes the situation crystal clear not only to the students involved in the disruptive event but to others who may be influenced to join in. There are practical examples of these correction sets in behaviour management texts such as *Comprehensive classroom management: Motivating and managing students* (Jones and Jones, 1995).

At times students will behave unsafely and lose self-control. Such situations are *not* behaviour management issues; they call for damage minimisation and protective behaviours. In situations such as these teachers should seek help immediately, stop teaching and focus on keeping three sets of people safe. These are the focus student or students, the other students and themselves. The order in which teachers do this is situation-specific. For example, if a student is about to jump out of a second storey window, he or she is the first to be protected. If a student is attacking others, focusing on protecting these others takes priority. If a student acts aggressively against the teacher, he or she should do whatever practical to remain safe. Teachers sometimes have to quickly remove the rest of the students from the class, and this is more easily achieved if they haven't wasted their authoritarian voices on irritating minutia.

Below are some key points to follow when working with students who are out of control. Teachers should:

1 Send for help immediately.
2 Remain outwardly calm.
3 Ask, 'What do you want?' instead of giving an instruction.
4 Avoid direct eye contact.
5 Signal or instruct other students to move away.
6 Put more space between themselves and the student.
7 *Discretely* remove potentially dangerous objects.

After a crisis event it is important for teachers to debrief with supportive colleagues, drink something sweet and consciously control their own breathing before continuing with their day or driving a car (vignette 3).

Shortly after handling a particularly challenging crisis at a behaviour unit with superficial calm, I experienced shock while driving home. It was a memorable experience; I don't recommend it. This had nothing to do with my small physical status or my gender; bodies are chemical factories that don't necessarily co-operate after being flooded with adrenalin.

Vignette 3 After managing a crisis

Figure 7 contains a protocol illustrating where crisis management sits. This protocol can be used to design a:

▶ single case intervention
▶ classroom behaviour plan
▶ behaviour management plan for event such as school camp
▶ and inform a whole-school behaviour management plan.

It is useful when designing single case intervention to begin with those behaviours that prevent the student connecting successfully with the curriculum, and flip those into goal behaviours. For example, 'The student punches'; this behaviour is transformed into the positive goal: 'The student keeps his hands to himself'. I recommend teachers make a huge effort never to speak of the disruptive behaviour again. When confronting the student it is useful to say, 'You had difficulty keeping your hands to yourself', rather than 'You punched'. This subtle difference trains teachers and students to focus on the goal in a relentless way.

Monitoring a student's progress towards these goal behaviours provides evidence for judging whether or not the student is more on task (or more co-operative) or not. However, it is vital that teachers relentlessly return to the student's strengths to remind them of their potential to achieve. This is difficult work and requires a mind-set that does not include giving up. Every student who is in distress has the potential to achieve more self-control and be more on task. It is a matter of finding the entry point and a way of communicating on common respectful ground. This takes time and concentrated effort. None of this good work is ever wasted.

CONCLUSION

When managing behaviour, teachers have to search their own hearts to employ the same generosity of spirit that they might hope others display when working with their own children, future children or grandchildren. I invite teachers to treat the enormous amount of influence they have over the climate of acceptance, or non-acceptance, in their classrooms with deliberate attention. Modelling is everything; influence begins and ends there. Teaching is the greatest profession of all, and sensitivities embedded in conversations when conflicts arise provide opportunities for all to practise respect at a practical level. These students are the products of our complex society; therefore it is up to elders in school communities to lead the way to peaceful coexistence.

What teachers can thoughtfully and practically give to this fraught area of behaviour management practice is improvement over time. This can be quietly achieved with the minimum of fuss if educators practice small changes relentlessly and reflect on the mistakes they inevitably make in the intensely personal work of teaching. Mistakes are essential in this – and in any other – learning challenge.

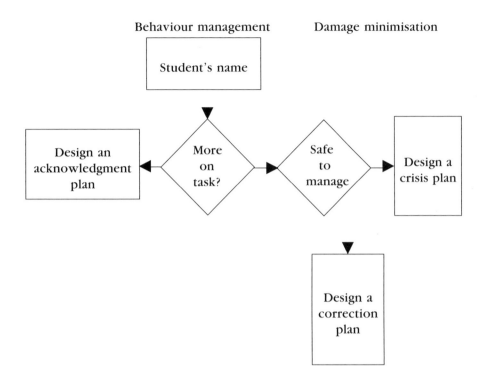

Figure 7. A useful decision-making protocol

There are two kinds of mistake to be made in the acquisition of an informed behaviour management repertoire: big ones and little ones. Little ones are those we know we make and big ones are those we refuse to acknowledge, and entrench through uncontested habitual practice so they become enshrined in our personal style. Big mistakes involve us attributing blame where it does not belong. I invite teachers to grow beyond some of their colleagues, to be brave, to take intelligent risks and to be prepared to 'humiliate' themselves in front of some of their less generous peers by advocating the education of even the most difficult-to-manage students. As one of my teachers, John Elkins of the University of Queensland, said, 'When our schools learn to teach the most challenging and challenged students well, conditions will be better for all.'

REFERENCES

Alberto, E. S. and Troutman, A. C. (1995) *Applied behaviour analysis for teachers* (4th edn.). Columbus, Ohio: Merrill.

Balson, M. (1996) *Behaviour management*. Keynote address. Cluster Staff Development, Marsden State High School.

Byrne, B. M. (1994) 'Burnout: Testing for the validity, replication and invariance of causal structure across elementary, intermediate and secondary teachers.' *American Educational Research Journal* 31: 645–673.

De Bono, E. (1998) *Simplicity*. London: Viking.

Elkins, J. (1994) Keynote address. Australian Association of Special Education, State Conference, University of Southern Queensland.

Jones, V. F. and Jones, L. S. (1995) *Comprehensive classroom management: Motivating and managing students* (3rd edn.). Boston: Allyn & Bacon.

Kaplan, J. S. (1996) *Beyond behaviour modification: A cognitive-behaviour approach to behaviour management in the school.* (3rd edn.). Austin, Texas: Pro-Ed.

Rogers, W. A. (1993) *The language of discipline: A practical approach to effective classroom discipline*. Plymouth: Northcote House.

5

So it's your fault! Defining the responsibilities of teachers, parents and students

Andy Miller

This chapter addresses the crucial links between home and school with regard to the management of students with emotional-behavioural disorders.

Consistent with recent DfEE (UK) guidelines about home-school links, Andy Miller and his colleagues have researched the nature and extent of home-school understanding and support for management of behaviour at school. Over several studies, Andy and his colleagues have focused on the perceptions of key stakeholders (parents, students and teachers) regarding the utility, viability and effectiveness of intervention and support strategies carried out at the school level. He outlines the practical implications for schools in their policy and practice. His research is optimistic about the effectiveness of supportive links between home and school and will encourage teachers to be more proactive in this crucial aspect of whole-school management.

A significant theme running through recent legislation and policy in the UK concerning behaviour in schools has been the continuing attempt to define the relative responsibilities of parties such as schools, local education authorities (LEAs), parents and students themselves.

In 1994, for example, a government circular required schools to develop and clarify their internal policies and procedures regarding student behaviour (DfEE 1994). This was then followed by a prescription placed on LEAs to confirm and make clear their co-ordinating role by means of published LEA Behaviour Plans (DfEE 1998).

Attention switched to the responsibilities of parents in a subsequent circular requiring all schools to draw up and adopt 'home-school agreements' (DfEE 2000a). This circular stated that respective responsibilities should be listed, including who should do what in terms of pupil attendance and behaviour, and then signed by both school staff and parents to indicate their intention to adhere to the contents. Government advice also added that these agreements would work best where they were 'a product of genuine discussion between all parties concerned' (DfEE 1998).

The strong emphasis on the rights and responsibilities of parents is also emphasised in Circular 10/99 (DfEE 1999) which states that schools should set up a Pastoral Support Programme for students experienced as particularly difficult to manage and in danger of being excluded from school. In this multi-agency programme, parents should contribute to strategy planning and 'be regularly informed about their child's progress'. Again, this government recommendation is founded on the belief that by making expectations explicit and agreed between school and home, more serious consequences may be averted.

THE EVIDENCE FOR HOME-SCHOOL APPROACHES

Although many difficulties and stumbling blocks are often encountered in attempts to implement home-school approaches to student behaviour problems, there is a strong evidence base for the effectiveness of these approaches, if they can somehow be arranged. The research has shown that very positive outcomes can be achieved by the use of strategies that basically require teachers to specify classroom rules, decide whether these have been followed and then communicate this information supportively and clearly to a pupil's parents. At home, parents are responsible for consistently dispensing previously agreed rewards and sanctions to their child, based on the teacher's information communicated to the child's home.

These strategies also include features such as: small achievable steps; criteria for moving between steps; rewards and sanctions; methods for ensuring consistency; and a jointly agreed recording system for exchanging information between home and school.

In the USA context, Barth (1979) and Atkeson and Forehand (1979), have reviewed a substantial body of published research demonstrating that, if it is possible to set up these types of strategies, then extremely effective outcomes can often ensue. Similarly, in the UK, Miller (1996) reported on 24 case studies of successful interventions in primary schools, some involving students described by their teachers as the most difficult they had ever encountered.

However, we all know that strong feelings of blame, hostility and a 'lack of co-operation' can easily become unleashed on occasions when student behaviour is considered to be a significant issue of concern and the barriers to arriving at a joint home-school strategy can seem insurmountable. For example, in a large-scale research project aimed at helping secondary-age pupils displaying challenging behaviour, Kolvin *et al* (1981) found that joint teacher-parent approaches could be characterised by 'mutual distrust and prejudice'. Similarly, Dowling and Taylor (1989), offering an advisory service to parents within a London primary school, concluded that '...the seemingly humble goal of reopening communication between parents and teachers must not be under-estimated'.

THE EXTENT OF SUPPORT FOR HOME-SCHOOL APPROACHES

Given this potential minefield, but also the research outcomes (in the literature) for those home-school strategies that are implemented, this chapter now turns to a series of research studies that have attempted to get beneath the surface of these issues and understand those psychological processes that really determine whether a strategy will be doomed to failure before it has begun, or whether it will receive initial and continuing support of a cautious or enthusiastic nature.

Much of the research on which this chapter is based is drawn from The Psychology of Behaviour in Schools Project which is being carried out at the University of Nottingham. This project involves practising educational psychologists and those in training working alongside teachers, students and parents in a range of research and practice initiatives, including individual casework approaches, group work with both teachers and students, and organisation development activities with senior managers in schools.

STUDY 1: HOW OPTIMISTIC ARE TEACHERS AND PUPILS ABOUT THE LIKELY SUCCESS OF HOME-SCHOOL STRATEGIES?

This piece of research (Miller and Black, 2001) set out to provide some answers about the optimism and enthusiasm with which pupils and teachers might support interventions involving teachers and parents working together. Clearly, if teachers are found to be pessimistic about the potential benefits of such strategies, then these interventions are unlikely to be used in classrooms. Equally, if pupils are unconvinced of their merits then they may resent a teacher's time being spent in this way, or feel that difficult pupils are being preferentially treated, thus causing additional difficulties and dilemmas for a teacher. In summary, if home-school approaches are to be used to their full effect, we must first know whether teachers and pupils feel they will bring about desirable results whilst treating each of the various parties involved in a fair and open manner.

Sample

The pupils in this study, 206 in total, were drawn from three primary schools in the north of England and were aged 10 or 11 years old. The study also involved 30 teachers from seven different primary schools.

Method

A vignette was constructed, based on two real and successful interventions from the Miller (1996) study, and was read out to class groups in stages. Between each stage, the students were asked to complete certain sections of a questionnaire. Exactly the same materials and procedures were used with the teachers, with some completing the task as a staff group and others participating individually with the researcher. The vignette was presented in stages in an attempt to approximate real-life scenarios, where interventions are launched without any certainty as to what will happen next. Decisions made as an intervention unfolds are therefore based on information existing at that time, rather than with the benefit of hindsight when outcomes are known. The case study in the vignette was presented in a very brief form but contained elements such as the recognition of strong and difficult emotions, teachers and parents being brought together by an educational psychologist, and clear statements about targets and rewards.

Results

This is the first section of the vignette read out to the teachers and pupils:

> *John is a 10-year-old boy who usually arrives at school late. He finds learning difficult and doesn't do much work. When he is given work that he can't do, he pushes it across the table and refuses to do it. When he is able to do it, he thinks it must be too easy and again pushes it across the table.*
>
> *John's teacher finds having John in the class very difficult. Instead of working, he wanders around the classroom hitting other children and banging objects together. His teacher finds it hard not to lose her temper with him and she gets very frustrated. John is quite aggressive to teachers as well as to children. If people don't do what he wants them to do, he can 'blow up': even throwing chairs around and running out of the classroom. In fact he often leaves the school as well. His teacher feels that she doesn't get much support from his mum and dad as they don't go up to school much and she hardly ever sees them.*
>
> *John's mum seems very protective of him. In her eyes John never seems to do anything wrong. John's dad has just come out of prison.*

A question was also asked to determine how severe the teachers and pupils judged John's behaviour to be. After the presentation of the first section of the vignette, they were shown a rating scale in which '1' stood for the 'worst behaved' student they had ever known, and '10' for the 'best behaved', and then asked to mark the place on the scale where they felt John's behaviour placed him. The results from this and subsequent ratings are shown in Table 1.

Also at this stage the teachers and pupils were asked which of the following people they thought had the most potential to bring about an improvement in John's behaviour: parents, teachers, John himself, other pupils or someone else?

The replies to this question are summarised in Table 2.

After replies to these questions had been marked on the questionnaires, the second section of the vignette was read out:

The educational psychologist came to the school a few times to sit in John's class and watch what was going on. One of the times she came to the school, she had a joint meeting with John's mum and dad and his teacher. As somebody who didn't usually work at the school, she was not so close to what was going on, and so she was able to listen to all sides of the story (mum and dad's views and the teacher's view). She made sure she really understood what they were all saying. It was clear that John's parents did not want him to go to a special school.

The educational psychologist made some suggestions to John's parents and his teacher of the things they could try at home and at school in order to help John. Together they worked out a behaviour plan. The plan involved John's teacher choosing three of the classroom rules for John to try to concentrate on. She chose: 'put up your hand, work hard and listen carefully'. She told John which rules she had chosen and explained that at the end of each lesson, they would sit down together and talk about how well he'd managed to stick to these rules. He would get 1 or 2 ticks depending on how well he had done. If he hadn't stuck to the rules at all he wouldn't get any ticks for that lesson.

John was keen to try this behaviour plan and very confident that he'd be able to get lots of ticks.

At the end of each week John and his teacher would count up the ticks, and if he had enough of them he would be allowed to choose where he wanted to go and work, for example to go and use the computer.

The ticks also went into a home diary, which John took home at the end of each week to show his mum and dad. They looked at the diary to see how well John had stuck to the rules by counting his ticks. When he had lots of ticks his mum and dad allowed him to do certain things he wanted to do. They also paid him 5p for each tick he got (though the school didn't know about this). Since the start of the behaviour plan, John's mum would go up to school quite often to say how pleased she was that he got so many ticks for a particular day.

After this second section of the vignette had been presented, the teachers and pupils were given another identical 10 point scale and asked to imagine the likely effect of this intervention on John's behaviour and indicate the rating that this would probably deserve. These findings are shown in Table 1.

When the ratings scales had been completed, the much briefer third section of the vignette was presented:

When the behaviour plan was being used, John's behaviour in classroom improved a lot.

A third rating was then made in the same manner with the teachers and pupils asked to imagine John's likely behaviour one month after commencement of the strategy, and then a fourth estimate based on the hypothesised state of affairs in six months' time. The results from these final two ratings are also displayed in Table 1.

Table 1. Teachers' and pupils' predictions of the probable degree of success likely to derive from the presented strategy

Rating scale: 1 = worst behaved pupil I have ever known,
10 = best behaved pupil I have ever known

	Teachers	Pupils
First section of vignette *Description of 'presenting problems'*		
A. How well behaved is John at school?	2.77	1.87
Second section of vignette *Outline of intervention*		
B. How do you think John will behave now?	4.93	6.08
Third section of vignette *Brief account of short-term outcome of intervention*		
C. How do you think John will behave after one month of the behaviour plan?	5.82	7.98
D. How do you think John will behave after six months of the behaviour plan?	5.83	9.67

Table 2. The number and percentages of teachers and pupils choosing either parents, teacher, John himself. other pupils or someone else as the person most able to help improve John's behaviour

Person chosen as being most likely to be able to improve behaviour

	parents	teacher	John himself	other pupils	someone else
Pupils' choices	79 (38.5%)	24 (11.7%)	57 (27.8%)	22 (10.7%)	23 (11.2%)
Teachers' choices	8 (26.7%)	13 (43.3%)	2 (6.7%)	0 –	7 (23.3%)

Conclusions

The findings presented in Table 1 give considerable grounds for optimism about the acceptability of these types of home-school strategies amongst teachers and pupils, and reveal a firm belief that they would produce beneficial outcomes. Both groups rated the original description of John's behaviour as severe, the pupils more so than the teachers (this difference being statistically significant). After hearing an outline of the strategy used, both groups also predicted distinct (again statistically significant) improvements in the short term. Whilst some of the positive expectations felt by the pupils in the longer term may be put down to a certain level of naivety, these findings do give good grounds for seeing other pupils as 'hidden resources' (Leyden, 1996); ready, willing and able to play a part in working towards solutions. The frequently voiced concern by teachers that pupils are likely to resent or suffer in some way from interventions aimed at other pupils displaying difficult behaviour is not therefore supported by the current research. And, whereas lower teacher expectations may reflect a more seasoned and cautious stance, it must be emphasised that *the teacher group did also become significantly more optimistic about the likelihood of success* once they had received an outline of the strategy.

The findings in Table 2 invite a little more caution, in that important differences can be detected in terms of the people that teachers and pupils see as having the most potential to bring about positive outcomes. Whilst 43% of teachers see themselves as being this person, pupils see parents and the particular student himself, rather than teachers, as having far more influence in bringing about success.

Although these differences need not constitute serious impediments to agreement upon a strategy and its successful implementation, they do raise a small note of caution – one which will be amplified in following sections of this chapter. Namely, if other differences between teachers, pupils and parents are found in these types of judgments, then the scene could be set for clashes of perception and belief with the power to bring down the best laid plans, however convincing the research evidence base and however severe the 'legislative strictures'.

WHY ARE HOME-SCHOOL APPROACHES NOT THE WIDESPREAD SUCCESS THE RESEARCH EVIDENCE SUGGESTS THEY DESERVE TO BE?

The discussion in this chapter so far has shown that recent legislation has required teachers and parents to work together over issues of difficult student behaviour and that such approaches are supported by a respectable research evidence base. Further, teachers and pupils have been shown to be fairly optimistic supporters of such approaches. In light of this, why is behaviour in schools still widely seen as such a pressing and seemingly irresolvable problem?

What is preventing a wider take-up of home-school approaches?

Answers such as time pressures in schools, a lack of co-operation from parents and anxiety about generating further strong and destructive feelings, all suggest themselves. There is another area, however, not yet examined, that may hold an important key: the beliefs that teachers, pupils and parents have about whom or what constitutes the cause of difficult behaviour in the first place.

Within the discipline of psychology, attribution theory seeks to investigate and understand how individuals invoke causes and explanations for various phenomena. In the case of difficult student behaviour, many types of explanation may suggest themselves. For example, some may seek to explain the origin of a student's difficulties in terms of social, economic or political pressures on schools, parents and pupils. Others might look to characteristics of the student – academic ability, attitudes, personality – or to factors such as the lifestyles or educational experiences of parents. Yet again, explanations may be sought in areas such as school policy or teachers' classroom management skills.

Attribution theory does not concern itself directly with tracking down the *true* or *real causes* of a phenomenon but, rather, examines the ways in which these perceived causes are arrived at. It is often on the basis of our attributions, rather than any 'objective truth', that we usually have to function in complex and fraught social situations such as these. Consequently, the remainder of this chapter will look in detail at what we know about the ways that teachers, pupils and parents make sense of the causes of difficult behaviour in schools, in order to learn more about what is really required to launch successful strategies from within schools.

STUDY 2: WHAT DO TEACHERS SEE AS THE CAUSES OF DIFFICULT BEHAVIOUR IN SCHOOLS?

In a survey of 428 junior class teachers, Croll and Moses (1985) found that behaviour or discipline problems were seen to be due to home factors in 66% of cases, to 'within-child' factors in 30% of cases, and in less than 4% to any school or teacher factors (including previous schools or teachers). Similarly, the Elton Report (1989) commented that:

> 'Our evidence suggests that teachers' picture of parents is generally very negative. Many teachers feel that parents are to blame for much misbehaviour in schools. We consider that, while this picture contains an element of truth, it is distorted.' (Elton Report, p 133)

In fact, after reviewing the pronouncements of a wide range of interested parties, Hood (1999) has argued that models of parents as 'problems' rather than 'partners' or 'consumers' are likely to dominate in situations where there is concern about student behaviour in school.

Results

Table 3. Teachers' attributions for the origins of difficult behaviour

Attributions made to:

Pupils	Parents	Teachers
need for praise (7)	general management of child (8)	interest level of work set (4)
lack of acceptance of social norms (7)	punitive/violent home (7)	work expectations/steps set (3)
'physical/medical' (7)	absence of father (6)	negative attention to pupil (2)
temperament/personality (6)	lack of attention to child (6)	teacher's anxiety (2)
not feeling valued/self-esteem (5)	divided loyalties re separation/divorce (4)	lack of incentives/tangible rewards (1)
attention-seeking (4)	management of difficult behaviour (4)	lack of record-keeping (1)
lack of acceptance of school rules (4)	geographical problems re separation/di-	lack of specific management techniques (1)
lack of maturity (4)	vorce (1)	lack of affection/sympathy for child (1)
attention span (4)	lack of encouragement (1)	teacher not making an exception (1)
lack of motivation towards school work (3)	atmosphere of disharmony (1)	pressure from other parents (1)
intelligence (2)	adoption issues (1)	
lack of awareness of effect on other children	parent illness (1)	
(2)	grandparents' influence (1)	
knowledge of specific school rules (1)	lack of affection (1)	
knowledge of general social norms (1)	house move (1)	
lack of respect for teacher (1)	geographical isolation (1)	
comprehension level (1)		
lack of awareness of effect on parent (1)		
'tough-guy' self-image (1)		
'clutter in head' (1)		
lack of trust in others (1)		
effect of bad previous school experiences (1)		

79

Clearly such unvoiced attributions have the potential seriously to undermine the quest for 'agreed and explicit' strategies devised in a spirit of 'genuine discussion' between teachers, parents and pupils. The research study presented here consequently sought to get beneath the surface of descriptions such as 'home factors' or 'within-child' explanations and to explore the more 'fine-grained' detail of the attributions that teachers make about causes (Miller, 1995).

Sample

This study was carried out with 24 primary school teachers, drawn from a wide geographical area within England. All of these teachers had in common the fact that they had collaborated successfully with an educational psychologist in implementing a strategy to manage the difficult behaviour of a pupil in their class.

Method

The investigation took the form of an intensive interview with each teacher and, as part of the analysis, the interview transcripts were subsequently 'combed' for all suggested or hypothesised causes of the original behaviour. All of these are listed in Table 3 with the number of teachers making each attribution shown in parenthesis.

Conclusions

Perhaps the most striking aspect of Table 3 is the number of different items it contains. Unlike some political pundits and sections of the media, these teachers clearly perceive causation to be a complex issue, influenced by a web of characteristics belonging to parents, teachers and pupils themselves.

However, there is another, less immediately obvious feature of these lists that has significant implications for this practice, and that is the extent to which these possible causes are seen to be under the *control* of the parties to whom they are attributed. If, for example, people were to view a student's 'attention span' as something beyond that young person's conscious control, then they would be likely to be relatively sympathetic towards any difficulties arising from this. Alternatively, however, behaviour judged to be within conscious control, perhaps a parent's 'lack of attention to a child' or a teacher's 'lack of record-keeping', is far more likely to elicit feelings of blame and disapproval.

The lists in Table 3 were examined item by item by a group of seven primary school teachers training to become educational psychologists. They were asked to make judgments about the degree to which each item might be considered to be under the control of the 'actor' to whom it had been attributed. When only the items commonly agreed as being highly within the control of each actor were compared this way, then a clear majority of the difficult behaviour was found to have been judged the *fault* of parents (Miller, 1995).

Despite the increasing official focus on partnership with parents, the repeated finding that teachers view parents as the major cause of a child's classroom misbehaviour, is likely to present a major stumbling block. Government advice on home-school agreements is unlikely to be received in the spirit intended when set against these widespread attributions towards parents.

STUDY 3: WHAT DO PUPILS SEE AS THE CAUSES OF MISBEHAVIOUR IN SCHOOL?

Sample

In order to answer this question, a two-part study (Miller, Ferguson and Byrne, 2000) was carried out in an inner-city comprehensive school in the north-west of England. This involved a total of 125 year 7 pupils (predominantly 12 years of age), comprising essentially that entire group for the school.

Method

The study was carried out using a questionnaire about the possible causes of difficult behaviour in schools, the items for this questionnaire having derived from a number of prior small-group interviews. The students who generated the questionnaire items were selected by the Head of Year, and were seen by the researcher in four groups of between four and seven, for periods of between 40 minutes and an hour. These pupils were judged by their teachers as being representative in terms of ability, behaviour and gender. After defining the purpose and ground rules for the interviews, and addressing issues of confidentiality, the groups were asked to think back to their time in primary schools and to remember the types of misbehaviour they had witnessed, and perhaps engaged in. Primary (rather than secondary) school settings were examined because that is the sector examined by the corresponding research on teacher attributions. Discussion was then encouraged by means of a set of questions to encourage the students to think of all the possible reasons why there might be misbehaviour in schools. These discussions were tape-recorded and all the suggested reasons were written up on a flip chart, and further prompts were used in an attempt to make sure that *all* possible reasons had been elicited. In general, the discussion groups were able to list factors related to parents and families but were reluctant to elaborate upon them. Items concerning teachers and other pupils were, however, discussed and elaborated upon at length.

A questionnaire was then constructed incorporating all the possible reasons provided by the groups using, wherever possible, the actual terminology of the students. One or two items, such as the possibility of sexual abuse, were omitted from the questionnaire, despite being raised in each group, because it was felt that – presented on a questionnaire – they might cause distress or anxiety. The resulting questionnaire consisted of 27 items (as in Table 4, but presented in a random order) and the students were asked how important they judged each to be as a cause of difficult behaviour in schools. Each questionnaire item was rated on a 4 point scale (1 = very important; 2 = quite important; 3 = not very important; 4 = not important at all).

In the second part of this study all pupils from the year group who had not participated in the preliminary discussions, 105 in total, filled in the questionnaire. This was administered in class groups with the researcher reading out the questions one by one in each class, providing reminders about the method of responding, and encouraging students to ask about any items where the meaning might be unclear or ambiguous.

Results

The data obtained from this study were analysed by means of exploratory factor analysis and further details of the statistical analysis carried out may be found in Miller, Ferguson and Byrne (2000). In essence, this approach identifies clusters of items that are perceived by those completing the questionnaires as belonging together in some way as 'psychological entities'. Table 4 shows the four factors that emerged from the analysis.

Table 4. Pupils' perceptions of the cause of difficult behaviour in schools

Factor 1
Teachers shouted all the time
Pupils were picked on by teachers
Teachers did not listen to pupils
Teachers had favourites
Pupils were unfairly blamed
Good work wasn't noticed
Teachers were rude to pupils
Teachers had bad moods
Teachers gave too many detentions
Teachers were too soft
Pupils didn't like teacher

Factor 2
Other pupils wanted pupil to be in gang
Other pupils told pupil to misbehave
Pupil was unable to see mum/dad

Pupils were worried about other things
Pupils like misbehaving
Other pupils wanted to copy work
Pupils needed more help in class
Classwork was too difficult
Other pupils stirred up trouble

Factor 3
There were fights and arguments at home
Alcohol/drug abuse by family members
Parents let pupils get away with too much
Families did not have enough money to eat or buy clothes

Factor 4
Too much classwork was given
Too much homework given
Teachers too strict

Factor 1 was termed 'fairness of teacher's actions' and appears to attribute misbehaviour to injustices on the part of teachers. The second factor was termed 'pupil vulnerability' and reflects misbehaviour attributed to some children being vulnerable either to pressure from other pupils, their own emotional turmoil or difficulties with school work. The third factor was termed 'adverse family circumstances' and reflects attributions for misbehaviour being located with the families' inability to control their children and general family problems (e.g. financial hardship, drink, drugs, etc.). The final factor represents another teacher factor but this time reflecting on the 'strictness of the classroom regime' in terms of the amount of class and homework set and the rigour with which the teacher managed the class.

Further analysis of this data showed that these pupils rated 'teacher's unfairness' and 'pupil vulnerability' as statistically significantly more important causes of misbehaviour than either family problems or how strictly the classroom was managed. There were no significant differences between the results obtained from boys and girls.

Conclusions

The present study has shown students to attribute to teachers a significantly greater responsibility for pupil misbehaviour than that which they attribute to parents. This is a dramatically marked contrast to the findings from Croll and Moses (1985), in which teachers attributed pupil misbehaviour to home rather than school factors by a ratio of 17:1. It is also a finding which will be unpalatable to teachers and many involved with educational policy making.

STUDY 4: WHAT DO PARENTS SEE AS THE CAUSES OF DIFFICULT BEHAVIOUR IN SCHOOLS?

Given the drive for parents to be involved in genuine home-school agreements and in acceptance of some responsibility for their children's school behaviour, it becomes imperative to know whether their attributional styles will resemble more closely that of the teachers or of the students. In order to investigate this question, a study that paralleled many of the procedures from the study of pupils' attributions was carried out with parents in an inner-city primary school (Miller, Ferguson and Moore, 2002).

Method

This again consisted of two parts, the first being a series of intensive small-group interviews designed to elicit scenarios that would form the basis of the questionnaire. The second and main study, was a quantitative survey of parent attributions regarding pupils' misbehaviour in schools.

Three initial small groups involving 15 parents – 12 mothers and 3 fathers – were carried out in an identical manner to those in the previous pupil study, in order to elicit all possible causes of difficult behaviour in school as the basis for a new questionnaire. These group interviews eventually yielded 61 different items, including the 27 previously obtained from the small group discussions with pupils.

Two copies of the resulting questionnaire and a covering letter were then distributed to all 165 families represented in the school. Because the school drew upon a large Bengali speaking population, copies of the questionnaire translated into Bengali were sent out where appropriate. The researcher also spoke to all the children about the project in assembly the same day and asked them to encourage their parents to complete the questionnaires and to return them to school.

114 families returned either one or two questionnaires – a response rate of 69%. In total, 151 questionnaires were received, of which 144 were usable for analysis. Of these, 38 (26%) were completed by fathers and 106 (74%) by mothers. Among respondents, 9 (6%) described themselves as black, 27 (19%) as Asian of Bangladeshi origin and 102 (71%) as white.

Results

Although the full 61-item questionnaire was administered to the parent sample, the present analysis concentrates only on those items also presented to the pupils in the previous study to allow for a direct comparison between the two groups.

Factor analysis of the parent responses produces a three factor model. Factor 1 was termed 'fairness of teacher actions', as in the pupil study, and appears to attribute misbehaviour to perceived injustices on the part of teachers. The second factor was termed 'pupil vulnerability to peer influences and adverse family circumstances' and reflects a view of misbehaviour as originating with pressure from other pupils, or from families' inability to control their children, and general family problems (e.g. financial hardship, discord, absent parent). The final factor 'differentiation of classroom demands and expectations', comprises school-based elements related to the appropriateness of, and degree of, support provided in respect of the curriculum demands placed upon pupils.

The factor structures for pupils and parents reveal a number of interesting comparisons and contrasts (as in Table 5).

Conclusions

Table 5 reveals a number of interesting comparisons and contrasts which are discussed in detail elsewhere (Miller, Ferguson and Moore, 2002). Firstly, the same factor, 'fairness of teacher's actions', emerges from the study of both parents and pupils. For both groups this is also seen as one of the most prominent causes of misbehaviour. The two studies were conducted in cities about two hundred miles apart and this result cannot therefore simply be a reflection of local circumstances common to both groups. Secondly, a factor concerning 'pupil vulnerability' rates equally highly for both parents and pupils as a major cause of misbehaviour. However, this study also shows that, in contrast to pupils, parents do agree with teachers that certain adverse home circumstances can also be seen as a major cause of pupil behaviour in schools.

These findings may be interpreted as either a cause for optimism or for pessimism. Although teachers express a 'lack of parental support' as a major barrier to being able to implement successful behaviour plans (Miller, 1996), the present study shows that parents, more so than pupils, do concur with teachers over certain aspects of the influence of home background. Therefore, it should not be assumed that parents automatically start from a different set of beliefs than teachers in this respect. The converse, however, seems to be the case when it comes to considering the possible influences of teachers on the behaviour of pupils, with parents and pupils far more likely to share a common opinion concerning the influence of actions by teachers that they deem to be unfair.

It must be emphasised again that these studies do not establish the 'truth' of any particular perspective, but they do highlight the fact that conflicting attributional patterns – if not recognised and addressed in some way – have the potential to create enormous obstacles to the search for agreement in this contentious area. The findings from these studies focus down on the actual nature of these obstacles and thus illuminate more precisely the challenges to be addressed, or circumnavigated, in the process of setting up potentially productive joint strategies.

Table 5. The most important causes of misbehaviour deriving from factor analytic studies with parents and pupils

PUPIL FACTORS	PARENT FACTORS
'Fairness of teachers' actions'	**'Fairness of teachers' actions'**
Teachers shouted all the time	Teachers have favourites
Pupils were picked on by teachers	Pupils are picked on by teachers
Teachers did not listen to pupils	Teachers are rude to pupils
Teachers had favourites	Teachers shout all the time
Pupils were unfairly blamed	Teachers do not listen to pupils
Good work wasn't noticed	Teachers are too soft
Teachers were rude to pupils	Good worked isn't noticed
Teachers had bad moods	Pupils are unfairly blamed
Teachers gave too many detentions	Teachers have bad moods
Teachers were too soft	
Pupils didn't like teacher	**'Pupil vulnerability to peer influences and adverse family circumstances'**
'Pupil vulnerability'	
Other pupils wanted pupil to be in gang	Other pupils tell pupil to misbehave
Other pupils told pupil to misbehave	Other pupils wanted pupil to be in gang
Pupil was unable to see mum/dad	Families do not have enough money to eat or buy clothes
Pupils were worried about other things	Other pupils wanted to copy work
Pupils like misbehaving	Other pupils stirred up trouble
Other pupils wanted to copy work	Pupil was unable to see mum/dad
Too much classwork was given	Parents let pupil get away with too much
Classwork was too difficult	Pupils like misbehaving
Other pupils stirred up trouble	There were fights and arguments at home
'Strictness of classroom regime'	**'Differentiation of classroom demands and expectations'**
Too much classwork was given	
Too much homework given	Too much homework given
Teachers too strict	Teachers too strict
	Too much classwork was given
'Adverse family circumstances'	Classwork was too difficult
There were fights and arguments at home	Pupil needs more help in class
Alcohol/drug abuse by family members	Pupil doesn't like teacher
Parents let pupils get away with too much	Pupil is worried about other things
Families did not have enough money to eat or buy clothes	

WHAT ARE THE IMPLICATIONS FOR TEACHERS AND SCHOOLS?

The sequence of studies described in this chapter has drawn attention to the central importance of issues of attribution to understanding the frequently intransigent nature of difficult behaviour in schools. This area of psychological study could well be seen as the 'missing link' between legal and policy imperatives on the one hand and workable, 'real world', strategies on the other.

The major implications for teachers from these and related studies can therefore be summarised as:

▶ Teachers are able to achieve successful outcomes even with the most disruptive pupils, if a way can be found to implement certain types of home-school approaches.

▶ As a prerequisite for achieving these, teachers will need to be aware of the attributions that they make for the causes of difficult behaviour.

▶ Once made explicit, a way must be found to 'put to one side' these attributions.

▶ Teachers will also need to be aware of the attributions being made by pupils and parents, whether or not these are actually voiced.

▶ Similarly, ways must be found to allow all parties to step to one side of these attributions, in the quest for an acceptable strategy. Engaging directly with beliefs about blame and responsibility – debating, challenging or seeking to establish the one ultimate truth – are likely to be extremely counter-productive, whereas acting as if they do not exist can feel like dishonesty or a failure of nerve.

The barriers to setting up home-school interventions can appear huge and insurmountable. To ask a lone teacher to navigate successfully and lead others through this web of attributions is a tall order, especially on occasions when feelings are running high. Any individual who can do so should be applauded and looked to as a potential mentor to others.

Fortunately, there is a growing number of accounts of externally-led individual and group work with teachers in this area (e.g. Osborne, 1983; Stringer *et al* 1992; Miller, 1996 and Hanko,1999) and legislators, policy-makers and managers of individual schools need to recognise the existence and value of this trend.

Support from within school that is obtainable through the formal and hierarchical channels and informally among colleagues, as well as support available from outside agencies, will need to be based on a recognition that the issue of 'difficult behaviour' often gives rise to intense and unpalatable feelings. Rather than denying these, or labelling them as 'unprofessional', the climate within a school needs to permit their safe expression. However, the emphasis must be on *safe* expression – on promoting the recognition that attributions are always one particular way of making sense of phenomena, and that persistence with 'a desire to blame' will be counter-productive. Distinguishing between allocating blame and the desire to pursue the causes of phenomena out of a natural human curiosity is necessary to avoid the creation of a culture that saps morale and initiative in this contentious area.

As in most forms of potential human conflict, from international tensions through to strained personal relationships, effective mediation and mutually acceptable resolution cannot be left to chance. This chapter has argued for the crucial contribution that psychological research in topics such as attribution theory can have in helping translate the broad aims of legislation and policy into dignified and successful outcomes for all involved.

(I would like to acknowledge the contributions made to the ideas expressed in this chapter by my co-researchers Dr Eamonn Ferguson, Laura Black, Irene Byrne and Eleanor Moore.)

REFERENCES

Atkeson, B. M. and Forehand, R. (1979) Home-based reinforcement programmes designed to modify classroom behaviour: a review and methodological evaluation. *Psychological Bulletin* 86, 1298–1308.

Barth, R. (1979) Home-based reinforcement of school behaviour: a review and analysis. *Review of Educational Research.* 49, 436–58.

Coulby, D. and Harper, T. (1985) *Preventing Classroom Disruption. Policy, Practice and Evaluation in Urban Schools.* London: Croom Helm.

Croll, P. and Moses, D. (1985) *One in Five. The Assessment and Incidence of Special Educational Needs.* London: Routledge and Kegan Paul.

Crozier, G. (1999) Is it a case of 'We know when we're not wanted?' The parents' perspective of parent-teacher roles and relationships. *Educational Research* 41, 3, 315–28.

Department of Education and Science (1989) *Discipline in Schools. Report of the Committee of Enquiry Chaired by Lord Elton (The Elton Report).* London: HMSO.

Department for Education (1994) *Pupil Behaviour and Discipline.* Circular 8/94. London: DfE.

Department for Education and Employment (1998) *Circular 1/98 LEA Behaviour Support Plans* London: DfEE.

Department for Education and Employment (2000) *Home-school agreements. Guidance for Schools.* London: DfEE.

Dowling, E. and Taylor, D. (1989) The clinic goes to school: lessons learned. *Maladjustment and Therapeutic Education.* 7, 1, 24–8.

Hanko, G. (1999) *Increasing Competence Through Collaborative Problem Solving: Using Insight Into Social and Emotional Factors in Children's Learning.* London: David Fulton.

Hood, S. (1999) Home-school agreements: a true partnership? *School Leadership and Management.* 19, 4, 427–40.

Kolvin, I. *et al.* (1981) *Help Starts Here. The Maladjusted Child in the Ordinary School.* London: Tavistock Publications.

Leyden, G. (1996) 'Cheap labour' or neglected resource? The role of the peer group and efficient, effective support for children with special needs. *Educational Psychology in Practice.* 11, 4, 49–55.

Miller, A. (1995) Teachers' attributions of causality, control and responsibility in respect of difficult pupil behaviour and its successful management. *Educational Psychology* 15, 457–71.

Miller, A. (1996) *Pupil Behaviour and Teacher Culture* London: Cassell.

Miller, A., Ferguson, E. and Byrne, I. (2000) Pupils' causal attributions for difficult classroom behaviour. *British Journal of Educational Psychology* 70, 85–96.

Miller, A. and Black, L. (2001) Does support for home-school behaviour plans exist within teacher and pupil cultures? *Educational Psychology in Practice.* 17, 245–62 (2002).

Miller, R. A., Ferguson, E. and Moore, E (2002) Parents' and pupils' causal attributions for difficult classroom behaviour. *British Journal of Educational Psychology.* (In press.)

Osborne, E. (1983) The teacher's relationship with the pupils' families. In I. Salzberger-Wittenberg, G. Henry and E. Osborne (eds.) *The Emotional Experience of Learning and Teaching.* London: Routledge.

Stringer, P. *et al.* (1992) Establishing staff consultation groups in schools. *Educational Psychology in Practice.* 8, 2, 87–96.

6

As chaotic as a box of frogs? Teaching learners who experience emotional and behavioural difficulties

Tim O'Brien

Tim O'Brien uses a metaphor that will resonate with teachers when he describes a teacher's experience of managing challenging behaviour as akin to . . . 'a box of frogs'. Tim has worked for many years as a teacher and senior manager in schools for learners experiencing emotional and behavioural disorders. In this essay, Tim encourages us to re-examine and understand 'emotional and behavioural needs', and why some students behave in attentional, challenging and confronting ways. While he never ignores the normative stress and practical challenges of management and discipline with emotional-behavioural disorder, he offers insightful understandings of how we can more effectively lead such students in their learning and behaviour at school. At all times Tim encourages us to seek to thoughtfully work with the potential in the child and discusses the kind of teacher-leadership likely to realise that potential.

I once asked a group of 16-year-olds who were attending a school for learners who experience emotional and behavioural difficulties (EBD) what they would like to do on their final day at school. Initially, they asked me to make the choice for them. Eventually, they chose to spend their time at a local rescue centre for abandoned dogs. Psychologically, it is interesting to consider why they would want to choose such a place to visit at the end of their formal education.

I organised the visit. When we arrived, they were immediately interested in the details and descriptors that were attached to the kennel of each animal. One notice said ' . . . this dog will react very aggressively if shouted at'. Another dog had a warning sign attached to his kennel ' . . . easily aggravated . . . currently has to be kept away from other dogs'. The group responded sympathetically when they saw an unkempt dog who was apparently too anxious to come out of his kennel, ' . . . abused at an early age and needs a great deal of care and attention', said the sign. They talked with empathy about how terrible it must be to have the difficulties that these dogs experienced. As they were a group who had often been burdened and stigmatised by the labels they had received within educational systems, their discussion was illuminating.

When the group of learners (all of them male) were gathered together at the end of the visit, an employee asked if they had any questions. The first question was 'If there was a fight amongst all of the dogs which one would win?' The next question was 'Doesn't keeping some dogs apart from others make them feel upset or angry?' These questions could be seen to offer some indications as to how these learners make sense of their world, as well as providing an insight into how they view the concepts of inclusion and segregation. Although I raise these issues, it is not this aspect of the visit that I wish to give prominence to here. As we were leaving, the employee privately admitted that he had been extremely worried about the visit of this group. A friend had told him what he could expect from 'disturbed children' and warned him that this visit would be a nightmare. Consequently, he had negative preconceptions, expecting the learners to present with disturbing and aggressive behaviour. Here was a situation where a perceived failure could be reframed positively. They had failed to live up to his expectations and caused him to question what their 'problems' actually were because he had seen no evidence of them at all. For me, this highlighted how the label EBD can instil fear in people, can be driven by assumptions and can also be defined by knowledge that is gained from others as well as by individual perception.

Taking up his remarks, a colleague (who knew this group and was liked by all of them) talked of seeing them in a different light too. She had noticed a more reflective and sensitive side to their personalities. She said that the visit had been completely stress-free for her. She explained why this felt unusual, 'Normally, working with kids like this is...*as chaotic as a box of frogs*'. This visual metaphor warrants a brief exploration at this point. The image of chaos implies an attempt to find predictability or establish patterns and order in an inherently unpredictable and complex environment. The box seems to imply an associated need for containment. The choice of frogs is interesting. Frogs often feature in fairy tales. Bettleheim (1991) proposes, from a psychoanalytical perspective, that frogs are symbolic representations of the 'most primitive states of our being' (p101). The transition from tadpole to frog reinforces their low evolutionary and low-energy state rather than altering it to a higher state. I am sure that my colleague was not deliberately characterising the learners in this way, she appeared to be saying that teaching learners who experience EBD is almost always turbulent and organisationally complex. But does it have to be that way?

EXPERIENCING DIFFICULTIES

I deliberately refer to learners who 'experience' EBD. The story of the visit to the dog rescue centre demonstrates, amongst other things, that there are times when the elements of EBD that can so often be explicit do not make an appearance at all. Many teachers will recognise that this is not particular to learners in special provision; it can easily happen with learners who attend mainstream schools. So, in this case, what caused the difficulties to seemingly disappear? Maybe it was related to the fact that the activity was a chosen one that was intrinsically motivating. Or it may have been to do with the learners connecting with needs that they understood and being given an opportunity to show compassion. Some might suggest it was to do with the relationships of the teachers and learners who were involved in the visit. Perhaps an answer can be sought by examining the complex interrelationship between all of these factors and more.

When I was a teacher I used to find the use of the phrase 'he's alright with me' to be one that could depress a teacher in an instant. Having had a difficult time in a lesson, a teacher would honestly admit to a colleague that they were finding the behaviour of a certain learner to be a challenge. If they were unlucky, this colleague would respond by saying that the learner concerned did not cause any difficulties in their classroom – 'he's alright with me'. It was usually a male – and sometimes his behaviour – which was under scrutiny. With some of the teachers who said this I was never sure of the validity behind their statement. For other teachers I knew, and who I would not have expected to make such a comment, this did seem to be true. There are in fact some learners who are 'alright' with certain teachers just as they are 'alright' in certain contexts and settings. The first question that has to be asked is what are these teachers doing – in individual interactions, in their thinking, in their classroom and curriculum management, and in their interventions – when learners present with behaviour that is challenging? By 'challenging' I refer to behaviour that is preventing new learning from taking place. Within this definition I would include behaviour that presents as withdrawn and passive as well as behaviour that can be considered to be confrontational and aggressive. Another question that has to be asked addresses how their good practice can be passed on to colleagues.

I also choose the word 'experience' because this points to the interactive relationship between the learner and the environment in which they are learning. It reinforces the view that the learning environment and those who manage it can influence an emotional and behavioural difficulty. As a consequence, difficulties and their associated needs can be seen as long or short term and *alterable*, rather than being fixed and located solely within the learner. The difficulties that had resulted in this group of 16-year-olds spending most of their schooling in an EBD special school seemed to have miraculously disappeared, or at least been put on hold, whilst at the dog rescue centre. My proposition would be that for all of these learners there were times when their difficulties were not evident in school too, be it a special school or in the mainstream schools that they used to attend but had been excluded from. There would have been times when what they had in common with other learners, rather than what made them appear different and resulted in their labelling, was there for all to see.

Learners who experience EBD are increasingly included in mainstream schools. As a result, there are teachers in mainstream schools who find that they are encountering needs and difficulties that are far more complex than they have met with previously. The difficulties that seem to concern mainstream teachers most of all, in these inclusive schools and classrooms, are those which result in learners presenting with behaviour difficulties (Croll and Moses, 2000). The teacher sets the limits for inclusion within their own classroom. They do so within an interactive and recursive agenda involving personal, whole-school, regional and national systems. It cannot be assumed that mainstream education will benefit all learners (Hornby, 1999) but responsivity can increase the potential for inclusion to succeed. For some teachers, the increasing complexity of need and difficulty encourages them to become more responsive. They enjoy the challenge of exploring their own attitudes, values and beliefs. They learn from the 'hard case' systems and people that test their thinking (O'Brien, 2001). In this way they can ensure that their classrooms are inclusive rather than explosive.

TAKING A JOURNEY INSIDE MY HEAD

There is an interactive relationship between how a teacher understands behaviour and how they deal with it when it is challenging to them or to others. There are inherent problems when a behaviour difficulty is perceived as if it was not connected with a learner's, or a teacher's, learning state. It is almost as if behaviour becomes divorced from all aspects of learning, including emotional factors. This can lead to limited perspectives and promote wide-ranging assumptions about what is happening and what can be done about it. This is because our own perceptions of why people behave the way that they do will be influenced by our belief and value systems and our theories of behaviour and learning. Our theoretical framework will control our judgements about, for example, the severity, nature and motivation of a behaviour difficulty. This may cause us to dismiss or overlook any analysis of the powerful emotional grounding that we ourselves have had in different relationships, such as those with our own parents, siblings and partners. We might also look at the behaviour of others and disconnect it from our own behaviour towards them. This ignores the reciprocal nature of interaction. Therefore, when things go wrong in the classroom a teacher can search for evidence that supports assumptions about certain learners rather than looking at their own behaviour. They can also legitimise challenging behaviour as being a consequence of the personality traits or family circumstances of particular learners. We may find ourselves stuck in rigid patterns of thinking about behaviour and learning. This inhibits a teacher's ability to provide emotional differentiation. It also restricts the fluidity of thought that is vital in changing negative behaviour and promoting positive behaviour. Fluid thinking enables learning to move forward.

Models that are formulated inside a teacher's head will affect how they understand what is taking place in a challenging and problematic situation. When confronted by the challenging behaviour of a learner, the teacher will be answering questions about their personal and professional 'self'. Their answers, gathered at high speed, will be informed by a notion of how learners should behave. They will also be influenced by any emotional overload they carry about specific learners. A teacher will also ask questions that will help them to make sense of what is really taking place, what they see as the motivation for the behaviour; the intensity of the problem and how the problem might be solved (O'Brien and Guiney, 2001). The responses to these questions will affect intervention. At best they provide the teacher with information that enables flexibility and provides resolution, at worst they can result in the three Rs that most teachers try to avoid at all costs – revenge, retaliation and recrimination. All teachers need to be given time to consider what they think, why they think it and if their thinking enables themselves and others to change and develop. Dialogues between colleagues should be encouraged. Those professionals who teach learners presenting with challenging behaviour should be offered regular opportunities to explore their beliefs and hypotheses as to why some learners might behave in this way. This can be done as individuals and in teams, lessening feelings of isolation and improving collegiality.

I AM PSYCHOPATHIC

I was teaching in a mainstream school where a young man called Darren had been engaged in low-level behaviour that had become chronically irritating to a colleague of mine. It is these low-level behaviours that wear teachers down rather than, for example, one-off incidents that may be potentially dangerous. Darren had attended a special school when he was younger and had developed a reputation for being difficult with certain teachers in his current school. My colleague had asked for support and I was able to offer to co-teach with him. Within minutes of the lesson starting Darren behaved in a manner that enticed my colleague into going from placid to angry at breakneck speed. My colleague was about to ask Darren to explain his behaviour. Darren seemed to take the words from the teacher's mouth and said them aloud 'I know what you are going to say now . . . (imitating the teacher's voice) . . . why are you behaving like that?' The teacher did not react to the impersonation, instead he asked, 'How did you know that I was going to ask you that question?' Darren paused and with a sense of pride announced for all to hear, 'Because I am psychopathic'. I noticed my colleague's wry smile but he respectfully avoided any comments that would have humiliated Darren. Very quickly, Darren corrected this error, 'No, wait a minute . . . I mean I am telepathic'.

The irony here is that there would have been some teachers who would have claimed that Darren was right the first time – that this medical label would explain some of his behaviour over the years. This is because our views are dependent upon our own reference points as well as how we gain knowledge and understanding about learners and their difficulties – accepting that there are many ways of knowing and understanding. There are also many ways of answering questions about the reasons for a behaviour difficulty and they will be dependent upon which framework of reference you choose to adopt. Differing models provide us with a variety of routes for understanding behaviour, developing formulations, assessing and changing behaviour (Ayers *et al*, 2000). So, for example, if I adopt an ecosystemic perspective I may wish to begin by exploring the problems that are inherent within the systems and subsystems that a child is part of, such as school and family, rather than looking at what is wrong with the child. However, if I adopt a biological perspective I may wish to begin by exploring factors such as neurological dysfunction and how it can affect behaviour. There are tensions and ethical dilemmas between different perspectives. An example would be where one explanatory model may validate the prescribing of mood-controlling drugs to change the behaviour of a child, whereas a competing model may see this as a form of chemical restraint and propose education intervention as a different solution (O'Brien, 1996). However, differing models do not need to be seen in terms of their rivalry, as tensions can also be used in a creative and complimentary manner.

SO, WHY ARE YOU BEHAVING LIKE THAT?

What type of answers might certain learners give to the question 'why are you behaving like that?' Here are some that are worth reflecting upon, as is their generalisability:

▶ *I am looking for attention.*
  Although a learner might not overtly describe their behaviour in this way, this is often a reason given by teachers to explain why challenging behaviour occurs. In some situations the learner does not seem to mind whether the attention they receive is positive or negative – as long at they receive attention of some description. It is important to state that, although attention may well be a motivational factor behind challenging behaviour, there are times when it is not the main or only factor. There are also times when it may not be a factor at all.

▶ *I need to get out of here.*
  Removing yourself from a situation involves a constellation of skills that need to be processed and applied. There may be many reasons why a learner might want to leave the room but their emotional and behavioural difficulties can highlight some of the gaps in their repertoire of skills. Some learners may not have the social skills to exit from the situation and might remain unclear about the rules that are involved in doing so. They may not posses the sophisticated emotional skills that enable them to do so without confrontation. They may lack communicative skills and therefore could be reverting to what has worked for them in the past, namely, communicating their wish to escape through their behaviour.

▶ *I am bored.*
The aims and potential outcomes of the task may not be explicit enough for a learner to understand them. They may see no connection to what is on offer to them in terms of their learning and their quality of life or life experiences. They may find that they are not provided with enough cognitive and emotional challenge or they may be given too much challenge that begins with learning that is processed as being too difficult. This can cause reactions such as impulsivity, hostility and fear.

▶ *The work that we are doing reinforces a negative image of myself.*
In this context the responsibility for exacerbating the difficulty lies fundamentally in the hands of the teacher. Although in some contexts teachers may be under the restraints of a prescriptive curriculum that has been defined and validated by the government, the teacher still has the opportunity to plan their teaching so that groups and individuals do not, unnecessarily, experience reinforcement of failure.

▶ *I have no power in my life so I will try to get some here.*
Some learners can feel an unrelenting sense of powerlessness. This can be brought on by factors which include family dynamics and history as well as how schools as institutions wield power over them. School, or particular classrooms, may be the only places that some learners can exercise power and feel empowered. In many cases the power is used instrumentally – without concern about the consequences that will follow. Being empowered is related with feeling a sense of belonging. It is helpful to consider what teachers can do to make a learner feel a real sense of belonging: feeling valued, listened to and respected.

▶ *I have an emotional and behavioural difficulty, so what can you expect?*
Any label can become pejorative and can identify the status of the person who carries it. When some learners are blamed for their difficulties their label is often used against them. In changing the self-concept of a learner there are times when a teacher has to make conscious and often exhausting efforts to prevent self-fulfilling prophecies from having the last word.

▶ *Attack is the best form of defence.*
Learners who experience emotional difficulties may well have egos that are fragmented and have become fragile because of negative episodes and damaging interactions in their lives. Psychodynamic theory proposes that all adults and children apply certain ego-defence mechanisms. Young people with emotional and behavioural needs may be more prone to projecting attributions that relate to their own self-concept onto other people. Some learners may have denied facts and experiences in their lives and when new experiences evoke related memories they might displace their emotions from one person onto another. In this context it could be the teacher who is the vessel for displacement. Thus behaviour can be the result of unconscious motivations and the teacher can be the recipient but not the cause of the

problem. These memories may cause regression and as a consequence a learner might present with behaviour that would not be expected from somebody of their chronological age. If this is the case, they need a teacher who supports them by consistently presenting with the behaviour that would be expected from an adult and a professional and not someone who reverts to their own regressive behaviours.

▶ *It is difficult being me and sometimes I cannot control what I do.*
This answer suggests that some learners do not have the self-regulatory skills to control their own subconscious impulses. They may not want to behave in a certain way but they just cannot prevent themselves from doing so. The development of self-regulation competence will improve a learner's ability to learn. Many of us will have found ourselves in situations where we have really wanted to say or do something but have engaged in introspective debate that enabled us to apply strategies to prevent us from doing so. We may also recognise situations where we feel that an emotion or emotional build up justifies a particular response that we would normally have kept under control. Imagine how difficult it must be for a young person who experiences emotional difficulties to deal with these internalised discussions and to develop coping strategies. Do you think that learners who present with challenging behaviour enjoy doing so and like being who they are in such situations?

I would propose that these answers, singly or in varying combinations, could be offered by most learners who can present with challenging behaviour in situations where they feel under threat, anxious or confronted by unpredict-ability. Those learners whose behaviour includes self-injury might add to the list that their behaviour – although it may have distressing outcomes – provides a form of sensory stimulation for them.

We can see that many of the answers show that the behaviour of a learner may not be personal towards the teacher at all. The act of depersonalising challenging behaviour is a key component of providing respectful intervention and can enhance the success of cognitive techniques such as conceptualising behaviour in terms of 'primary, secondary and residual behaviours' (Rogers, 2000). Through this process of clarification, challenging behaviour can be redirected and refocused so that positive behaviour can be affirmed and rewarded.

LEARNING NEEDS NOT BEHAVIOUR DIFFICULTIES

There are some teachers who are spectacularly able at teaching learners who experience EBD. How do they think and behave? They certainly never bear grudges against learners. Instead, they offer them a fresh start every day, or every lesson, or in some cases every few minutes! Instead of building barriers between teachers and learners, they build bridges. They constantly model the behaviour that they wish to see amongst the learners they are responsible for. In situations that become challenging what they say and do shows that they are not feeling threatened and nor are they a threat. They use respectful humour to diffuse situations that are in danger of escalating. They think in a fluid rather than a fixed manner. When teaching individuals or groups they use praise that is regular, specific, timely and sincere. They demonstrate to the learners that being fair means treating everyone differently – asserting individuality and diversity over sameness as well as highlighting positive reinforcement as an issue of equality of opportunity. They demonstrate a generosity of spirit, a willingness to be flexible, and revel in the riskier aspects of teaching and learning. Much of what they think and do can be passed on to colleagues through continuing professional development as well as within peer-support systems. In this way what they are offering to the learners does not disappear out of the door with them when they move on to work elsewhere. There will be many reasons as to why these teachers are so exceptional at what they do. My view is that one of the key features that makes them able to continue to work in such a positive manner is that they do not buy into the 'difficulties culture'.

In the UK, terms such as 'retarded' 'remedial' 'backward', or in relation to EBD, 'maladjusted' are no longer part of the acceptable language of educational systems. There are new labels which similarly cause us to make assumptions about where the difficulty is located and what its implications are for teaching, learning and inclusion in the wider community. These labels continue the trend of being markers of a person's difficulty. They focus on what is wrong with a learner or groups of learners, a deficit-model. The label can become a catalyst for the development of a culture of difficulty: where expectations become lowered, learners are seen as difficult and teaching them is seen in a similar light. Of course, we need to know what a learner's difficulties are and might be, but the teacher does not need to develop restrictive and negative orientations, otherwise hopelessness can become endemic. Teachers who excel when working within the context of EBD are analytical about difficulties and use them to focus upon *needs*. That is a key difference. Their thinking does not become static when they encounter a difficulty. It is what the difficulty says about the needs that they are interested in as that will help them to decide what provision should be put in place.

When looking at the needs of a specific learner, a teacher will consider what each learner has in common with everyone else as well as what makes them unique. When considering students' needs the teacher is able to reflect upon critical factors within the learning environment, which includes the home. This provides information that will have a direct influence upon how to teach and develop relationships with learners and their families. A needs-focus allows the teacher to consider how power can be shared and how learners can be supported in changing their behaviour. This is a very different approach than one of being wrapped up in what has gone wrong for a learner, their overwhelming difficulties and how difficult it is, and will be, to teach them. A focus upon needs is positive as, through the process of our thinking, a behaviour difficulty can be conceptualised as a learning need. Once the need is identified and focused upon the teacher can actively mediate a change in a learner's behaviour. This should not be confused with the teacher actually making the change – it is the learner who makes the change. When positive changes occur, the persons involved in mediating the change should ensure that those who have made the change are rewarded.

INTERVENTION OR INTERFERENCE?

An intervention enables a teacher and learner to think and act differently; to change people and environments for the better. Every teacher-learner interaction could be seen as an intervention. However, it is worth remembering that learners, like teachers, differentiate between the interactions that they are involved in. There are those in which their involvement is active and negotiated and the benefits are clear, whereas others are perceived as highly intrusive and an invasion of privacy. This is the difference between intervention and interference; the latter often involving strategies that can result in loss of dignity. Intervention is grounded in learning needs and the experience of the learner. It considers more than simply the point of view of the person who is carrying out the intervention – that is interference. In any difficult situation where intervention has taken place – when it ends (and it will end) – a teacher will have found a way out for the learner and the teacher. The teacher will have remained focused upon what a resolution might look and feel like and will have helped to eliminate or alleviate challenging behaviour. Schools have to establish consequences for behaviour that is deemed to be unacceptable and they can be applied reflectively, ethically and according to the agreed principles of school policies. Consequences are an important element of school life. Learners need to know that they exist and will be applied. When they happen they can still remain part of a positive ethos in that they can show that a person can be respected while their behaviour is being rejected.

Respectful intervention or disrespectful interference will be evident in how teachers behave when things do go wrong in the classroom. In these situations a teacher can find themselves in a 'learning zone' or a 'battle zone' (O'Brien, 1998). Suddenly finding yourself in this situation presents the teacher with the likelihood of being reactive to difficulties rather than responsive to needs. This is why the process of thinking about learning and behaviour is vitally important. It enables a teacher to have a mental plan of how resolutions can be achieved. This plan can become effective when it incorporates a thoughtful range of strategies, such as tactical ignoring, offering 'take-up time' and applying considered questioning techniques (Rogers, 1998), but the thinking has to be done beforehand. Although the description of a learning or battle zone may caricature and polarise teacher responses it does demonstrate how teachers can ensure that they know how they intend to behave when things become difficult. This reduces the unpredictability of stressful situations. For example, a teacher may ensure that they do not provide learners with instruction clutter – a charter of 20 things to do in the next ten seconds or else the threat of the most severe consequences imaginable will be brought to bear. Instead, one or two clear prioritised instructions are given. They may also ensure that interventions are not driven by the status of the teacher or a desire for oppressive control. When this happens it can take the teacher into the battle zone and intervention becomes interference. The worst case scenarios escalate out of control once the teacher adopts sarcasm as a weapon to use against learners. The corrosive nature of sarcasm within relationships cannot be overstated.

Respectful, dignified and dignifying intervention will also offer 'feedback' and 'feedforward'. This makes intervention a process that involves cyclical rather than linear thinking. It provides continual opportunities for mutual learning rather than seeing any problematic incident as having a beginning and end with no further implications or repercussions for the persons involved. Feedback should not only involve opportunities to engage in the mirroring or reframing of the behaviour of the learner but also in identifying and assessing the feelings or actions that may have caused the challenging behaviour to occur. This explores and validates the subjective experience of the learner and the teacher. 'Feedforward' will concentrate on what the teacher and the learner can do together to reduce or prevent difficulties. This will include approaches that aim to develop emotional, cognitive, communicative and social skills so that those factors that could be maintaining challenging behaviour can be analysed and altered. Intervention by the teacher is reduced over time, but at the outset supporting a learner in changing their behaviour can be teacher-intensive. Here the role of the teacher taking an active role as the mediator, rather than facilitator, of change again comes to the fore.

'ONCE UPON A TIME . . .'

I would like to return to the imagery of the frogs that my colleague articulated and take another look at it in relation to fairy tales. In some of these tales frogs are reviled because they symbolise baseness, threat and even evil. However, they can become empowered so that their state of being changes substantially. Their involvement in maturing mutual relationships causes this to happen. Interestingly, this is one leap that a frog cannot make on their own – they need someone else to help them to do so. In relation to the frog, this key person always sees beyond superficial presentations and simplistic explanations; they consider what potential is and how it can unfold, and place trust and dignity at the core of the relationship. Exceptional teachers of learners who experience EBD also make their own leap – a leap of faith. Through their thinking and actions, stories about transforming to a new and higher state of being do not have to remain within the realms of fairy tales. They actually happen in classrooms.

REFERENCES

Ayers, H., Clarke, D. and Murray, A. (2000) *Perspectives on Behaviour: a Practical Guide to Intervention for Teachers* (2nd edn.). London: David Fulton.

Bettleheim, B. (1991) *The Uses of Enchantment: The Meaning and Importance of Fairy Tales.* London: Penguin.

Croll, P. and Moses, D. (2000) Ideologies and Utopias: educational professionals' view of inclusion. *European Journal of Special Needs Education.* 15 (1) 1–12.

Hornby, G (1999) Inclusion or delusion: Can one size fit all? *Support for Learning* 14 (4) 152–157.

O'Brien, T. (1996) Challenging Behaviour: Challenging an Intervention. *Support for Learning* 11 (4) 162–164.

O'Brien, T. (1998) *Promoting Positive Behaviour.* London: David Fulton.

O'Brien, T. (2001) 'Learning from the Hard Cases' in T.O'Brien (ed.) *Enabling Inclusion: blue skies... dark clouds?* London: The Stationery Office.

O'Brien, T. and Guiney, D. (2001) *Differentiation in Teaching and Learning: principles and practice.* London: Continuum.

Rogers, B. (1998) *You Know the Fair Rule and much more: Strategies for making the hard job of discipline and behaviour management in school easier.* Melbourne: ACER Press.

Rogers, B. (2000) *Classroom Behaviour: A Practical Guide to Effective Teaching, Behaviour Management and Colleague Support.* London: Books Education.

7

Current trends in the management of emotional and behavioural difficulties

Lynne Parsons

Inclusiveness in education has long been a stated goal in educational policy and practice. In this essay, Lynne Parsons seeks to show how this aim has been realised in her own school. Lynne Parsons has had considerable and extensive experience in behaviour management in her consultancy role in the LEA (Oxfordshire). She has now taken up headship of a learning centre at Bicester Community College, a secondary school in Oxfordshire. Lynne advocates a whole-school approach to behaviour management that extends to learning centres as 'inclusiveness centres' within a school. She discusses the practical challenges of setting up such a learning centre – the discipline, philosophy and practice from correction and sanctions through to individual learning and behaviour plans. This case study is a practical and very helpful example of how the goal of inclusiveness can be realised in a mainstream school setting.

After working as an advisory teacher in the field of emotional and behavioural difficulties for 10 years, being asked to set up a learning centre for disaffected secondary pupils presented me with quite a challenge. For the whole of the 1990s I had spent my time advising and supporting schools across Oxfordshire in managing and supporting pupils with emotional and behavioural difficulties. I had always believed that I was the kind of support teacher who was happy to 'roll my sleeves up' and support in a very practical and 'hands on' sort of way! Now I was going to have to 'put my money where my mouth was!' and demonstrate that I could do it for real. Challenge it was certainly going to be; poisoned chalice . . . ? I would have to wait and see. On the other hand, I also needed to remind myself that in the late 1970s I was teaching in what was then called an off-site unit attached to a mainstream secondary school. Now I was being asked to set up and manage a learning centre. In reality was there going to be a difference between the two, even with the greater emphasis now on inclusive education?

From the outset I was clear that I would utilise all of those positive influences that had informed my work as an advisory teacher. This would be my opportunity to demonstrate that the theories of behaviour management I had long proselytised could work in practice when consistently applied. I was also determined that I would be eclectic in my approach and not be hidebound by one particular model of behaviour management. I was convinced that, above all else, *consistency* coupled with *flexibility* was necessary to cope with, and support, the various and different needs of the students with whom I would be working. I was fortunate; the secondary school that had asked me to set up the learning centre was a school with which I had worked closely as an advisory teacher and they already had in place the kind of behaviour management practices with which I could empathise and build on.

THE IMPORTANCE OF WHOLE-SCHOOL APPROACHES

I had long been promoting the management of individual pupil behaviour in the context of whole-school behaviour policies. The importance of getting schools to understand that behaviour management was a bit like fitting together huge pieces of a jigsaw puzzle was paramount to me. Each piece had to fit 'snugly' with its surrounding pieces, and the wrong piece in the wrong place could affect the way in which behaviour was managed at every level. The model suggested by Galvin, Miller and Nash (1999) had worked very well for me in my work as an advisory teacher. This is a tiered approach to behaviour management that addresses pupil behaviour at three levels. Level one examines issues relating to whole-school policies. Level two encourages teachers to translate policy into practice in the classroom, and level three explores the kinds of initiatives schools can employ to support those individual pupils who are difficult to manage. The success of using this particular model is that it is then easy for the whole school staff to recognise the importance of having all three levels in place in order to have effective behaviour management strategies. It is vital that staff understand that effectively addressing the whole school issues is likely to minimise disruption in the classroom. Equally, successfully addressing classroom management issues is likely to minimise the number of individual pupil referrals. This three tier model leads into a whole range of practical in-service training sessions for schools that support them in developing their whole school policies.

At the first level I had encouraged senior management teams to develop exercises designed to support them in agreeing with the whole school community on their overall values and ethos. This included, for example, agreeing about how to celebrate achievement, how to encourage students to take responsibility for their own learning and agreeing criteria for fair and effective sanctions. Involving parents/carers in supporting their children, and agreeing how varying styles of teaching and learning could be used to enable students to get the most from the curriculum were of equal importance. Any learning centre developed to support staff and students would have to uphold the ethos of the school and encourage the students to respect its values, involve their parents/carers and create a learning environment that guaranteed success.

Much of the work I did as an advisory teacher was based around supporting schools in developing a classroom discipline plan (the second level of a whole-school approach). Schools were encouraged to develop rules, rewards and consequences to effectively manage behaviour in the classroom through a range of experiential workshop activities. Schools in Oxfordshire with whom I had been working were greatly influenced by the work of Bill Rogers, who had led an annual conference in the county for the past eight years. I had organised these conferences in the summer term each year as a way of celebrating the work that had gone on in the county in the field of behaviour management. It was an opportunity to share good practice, be inspired further and pick up new ideas to try out in the classroom the very next day. 'Promoting positive behaviour' became a catchphrase within the LEA and most schools were using this phrase to describe their approach to behaviour management. Another influence was the Assertive Discipline model brought to Oxfordshire as a result of a successful Standards Fund bid. Almost half the schools in Oxfordshire have teachers trained as Assertive Discipline leaders. As part of this training I had devised a workshop pack that enabled all newly trained leaders to deliver six hours of in-service training to their colleagues in order to introduce them to Assertive Discipline *Oxfordshire style*. Walk into many classrooms in Oxfordshire and you will be able to see a published classroom discipline plan, often signed by the students and teachers using that room.

One of the most powerful and effective strategies teachers practised at this level was developing a 'language of discipline' (Rogers 1993). This included giving instructions, offering praise and encouragement, issuing warnings and rule reminders when necessary, and most importantly, providing students with choices and the opportunity to make the right choices. This would provide me with the foundation stones of the learning centre. This second level was the means whereby I could model good practice in the learning centre for colleagues teaching in mainstream classrooms.

No matter how effective schools are at promoting positive behaviour at these two levels, teachers always want to discuss what systems and procedures could be put in place to support individual students experiencing difficulties. Most schools have sophisticated systems for developing individual education plans through the Code of Practice for Special Educational Needs. Links to the support of external agencies are usually well advanced. Developing formal peer support networks for teachers offered staff a forum for developing action plans to support individual pupils who were more difficult to manage (Hill and Parsons, 2000). However, I was frequently asked about supporting students for whom the normal school systems seemed to be inadequate. The dilemma was how to support both teacher and student whilst acknowledging the skills, expertise and professional judgement of the teacher, and also recognising and understanding the vulnerability and needs of the student. The seeds of how the development of a learning centre might fulfil the above criteria were beginning to take root, and it was this third level that I could see would provide me with the greatest challenges.

DEVELOPING LEARNING CENTRES FOR STUDENTS WITH EMOTIONAL AND BEHAVIOURAL DIFFICULTIES

After a period of some 15 years, learning centres, tutorial units (or whatever we decide to call them) are again in vogue (*Social Inclusion: Pupil Support*, 1999). In setting up a learning centre I was keen to avoid the pitfalls associated with tutorial units in the past. There were several issues that immediately sprang to mind. Firstly, it was very important that the learning centre was seen as an integral part of the school, and reintegration back into mainstream lessons, as and when appropriate, was, from the outset, a prime objective. Secondly, and related to my first concern, I thought it was vital that both staff and students felt a sense of ownership of the learning centre. This would be dependent on the kinds of relationships I was able to develop with both staff and students; a delicate balance of support and understanding but a firm resolve about what I wanted to achieve for the whole school community. Thirdly, I wanted the students, and parents of the students referred to the centre, to know that they were not being denied their entitlement to a broad and balanced curriculum. By the same token I wanted to provide them with something different and not more of the same where they had already experienced failure. Finally, it was my firm belief that I needed to create an atmosphere that was conducive to motivating, inspiring and encouraging disaffected young people to succeed, feel proud of their achievements and have the confidence to go on and achieve yet more. I wanted to create a positive atmosphere based on mutual trust and respect, and a welcoming physical environment that could be a model for the whole school community.

I was clear in my own mind that the one thing I had learned above all else as a result of the work I had done in relation to managing behaviour was that the development of excellent personal relationships was the cornerstone upon which everything else would be based. Research has already demonstrated that 'schools that consciously encourage good personal relationships were likely to experience fewer incidents of difficult behaviour' (Parsons, 1992). Good personal relationships would be paramount in creating an atmosphere in which the students would feel secure enough to try out what might or might not work in the mainstream classroom. Good personal relationships with parents would be crucial in creating the powerful home-school links crucial in reducing disruptive behaviour. And good personal relationships with staff would be the only way of moving forward if I was to be able to persuade and motivate staff to try out, in their own classrooms, the strategies that worked in the learning centre.

Although the secondary school had good personal relationships within the whole school community, they had high exclusion figures. Most recently a working party of teachers, learning support assistants, governors and students had developed a comprehensive behaviour policy. The senior management team then took a bold and imaginative decision to develop a learning centre for students who had already had more than one fixed-term exclusion or whose behaviour made it likely that they would be excluded. The primary purpose of this learning centre was to promote inclusive education for students with emotional and behavioural difficulties. This meant that the centre had to offer students the opportunity to be calm, to learn, to develop alternative ways of dealing with difficulties and, most importantly, to be able to return to mainstream classes.

Once I had been asked to set up and manage the learning centre I decided to base all the work that happened in the centre on the kinds of interpersonal skills promoted in Adlerian psychology. There are four phases to this model. The first phase entails establishing an empathetic relationship in which students feel understood and accepted. The next phase demands an exploration and assessment of the student's beliefs, feelings, motives and goals. The third phase involves interpretation and insights in order to support students in learning to perceive themselves and their situation in a different light. The final phase requires reorientation and action, to enable the student to consider alternative attitudes, beliefs and action, while encouraging a commitment to change (Hill and Parsons 2000). I had always emphasised to teachers how important it was to criticise the behaviour and not the child. I was now in a position to demonstrate to the whole school community at Bicester Community College how this simple (and yet complex) maxim could be applied to the behaviour of some of the most challenging students in the school. 'It is one of those simple but beautiful paradoxes of life: when a person feels that he is truly accepted by another as he is, then he is freed to move from there and begin to think about how he wants to change, how he wants to grow, how he can become different, how he can become more of what he is capable of being.' (Gordon 1970.)

THE 'STAR ZONE'

The Star Zone opened in September 2000, but not before staff at the school had been invited to enter an open competition to 'name the learning centre!' There was a prize for the winner and there were lots of entries. This immediately created a sense of ownership amongst the staff before we were up and running. It also created the idea that this was a project in which everyone had some investment. Senior management chose the winning name and the Star Zone was born. As the teacher in charge it was not the name I would have chosen but one year on, the Star Zone is now synonymous with support, safety, security and understanding. It stands for nothing in particular, but 'stars' leave the Star Zone to sparkle in mainstream lessons during the school day every day.

It was important to establish from the outset that the Star Zone was not a 'sin bin' and neither was it to be a place where students could be sent at the whim of individual teachers. My first task, therefore, was to develop a watertight referral system that was clear, simple to administer but flexible enough to deal with emergencies should they arise. All students referred to the Star Zone are on the special needs register and have emotional and behavioural difficulties as the primary concern. Some of these students have learning difficulties also. All of the students are at risk of exclusion from school and the majority have had one or more fixed-term exclusions. All members of the teaching staff, including learning support assistants, have a responsibility to raise concerns about individual students through subject departments and/or the year teams. Once a concern has been raised and discussed with the relevant staff, the head of year may choose to make a referral by completing a referral form. Once this has been received I assume responsibility for either convening a formal meeting or liaising with staff informally in order to ensure that the student is withdrawn from the appropriate subject or subjects. Parents are informed and invited to a meeting in school. They are provided with a tour of the Star Zone and given a short information leaflet explaining the purpose of the centre and its aims. This is the start of very close and regular communication with parents. Positive phone calls home are made at least three times a week and certificates of achievement are sent home weekly. Parents have then always been exceptionally supportive when the more negative phone call has to be made. I assume responsibility for maintaining and reviewing the students' individual education plans and statements of special educational needs, if appropriate. The regular contact with parents has, therefore, meant that there has been an increase in the number of parents attending review meetings and contributing written comments to the annual review of statements.

All students newly referred to the Star Zone have an induction meeting. This first meeting is very important for several reasons. Firstly, it is important to dispel some of the myths that inevitably grow up amongst the student population about a learning centre such as this. For example, the belief that no-one ever has to do any academic work and that you can play games all day long! Secondly, it is crucial that students appreciate that the Star Zone is an integral part of the school, and that the values and ethos of the school are the values and ethos of the Star Zone. At this induction meeting students are also asked to complete a sequence of tests. This includes a self-esteem test, three cognitive skills tests and a personal evaluation test. This last one enables staff in the Star Zone to assess what kinds of learning skills the student needs to develop further in order to maximise learning opportunities in the classroom. Each of these tests provides me with a baseline assessment of where students are in terms of their perception of self, their interpersonal skills and their attitudes toward school. It then becomes possible to monitor student progress in each of the areas and students are later re-tested as part of the reintegration process back into mainstream lessons. It also means that staff in mainstream lessons teaching Star Zone students can be given specific advice and strategies to support students. Informally this happens whenever I have discussions with staff about individual students at break times, after school or when staff drop into the Star Zone as they frequently do. Formally, discussions take place every half term at the special needs link meetings, when I might facilitate a peer support meeting to develop an action plan to support staff in managing the behaviour of an individual student. All staff are issued with a termly individual education plan for every student in the Star Zone that details the specific strategies necessary to support the student and an even more detailed newsletter is sent out at the start of each new term.

Over and above this all students referred to the Star Zone carry a Star Zone record card. At the induction meeting students are assured that they are not being 'put on report' with all the negative connotations this seems to have for students. The purpose of this card is to enable me to monitor student progress toward meeting their individual education plan targets as they move from lesson to lesson. It took time to persuade students that carrying a record card was not a sanction, but a positive way to support and encourage progress. During the first term of Star Zone's existence students frequently failed to get their cards signed, left them at home or simply did not consider them to be important enough to remember. They often languished at the bottom of bags or in coat pockets. Constant reminders, positive encouragement and a determination not to sanction those students who failed to maintain their cards have paid off. Now we rarely have occasions when record cards are not completed and shown to me at the appropriate times. Staff give students an A, B or C grade for each target at the end of each lesson. 'A' means the student has reached their target, 'B' means that the student has made some effort to meet their target and 'C' means that the student has made no effort to meet their target. These record cards are an invaluable source of information about student progress on a lesson-by-lesson basis, and are used to inform review meetings with parents, staff, external support agencies and education officers. Each student is also given a weekly tutorial to discuss their progress in relation to their targets and, if necessary, targets are altered to give more focus or changed to take account of concerns that the student, parents or staff may have. The best testament to the success of the use of these record cards is the visits from students between lessons to show me how well they are doing. Equally gratifying is when colleagues send students to the Star Zone to show off their work or record card. The record card is also a means whereby I can communicate with colleagues in school and parents, who are invited to add their comments as are the students.

Rewards and sanctions are an important way of supporting and encouraging students to behave well and learn effectively. The school had already established a reward system based on stamps and certificates and, in keeping with ensuring that the Star Zone was seen as an integral part of the school, I fully intended to make use of this system. However, I was also keen that the Star Zone had a reward system of its own; the question was: what could I use that was practical but sufficiently different and, at the same time, valued by the students? In the event I need not have worried. I have, ever since its inception, taken in a variety of stickers, certificates, engraved pencils and other tokens and the students choose their own rewards. The key is to maintain the variety. At the moment the favoured reward is some quite small translucent smiley face stickers that fit neatly onto the Star Zone record cards. Some students have been rewarded with trips out and there has always been a recognition by students in the Star Zone that those students have deserved it because of their extra effort and progress. Students making consistently good progress are rewarded with gift vouchers and their names recorded on a special wall chart.

It was more difficult deciding on Star Zone sanctions. I had always felt the demand for detentions resulted in increased confrontation. In the end I opted for consequences that related to the rule broken (Rogers 1990). If students waste time they make the time up, if students are impolite or abusive they apologise and if students throw bags or anything else across the room they are asked to pick them up. Sometimes the students do not like it but they have always seen it as fair and have co-operated for the most part. It sounds simplistic but it works because I am consistent and the students are certain that I will follow up. I believe that the rewards and sanctions I have developed are effective because they are based on the positive relationships that have been established and built on in the Star Zone. They are based on the respect I have for the students as individuals and the fact that they trust me and other staff working in the Star Zone to use both rewards and sanctions consistently and fairly and as a positive way of encouraging good behaviour and purposeful learning. All students referred to the Star Zone are aware that agreed sanctions will certainly be applied even if they do not seem to be that 'severe' (Rogers 1992). Keeping students back at the end of the school day for three minutes wasted time during a lesson is as powerful as it is effective, especially if that time is also used to mend bridges and repair relationships.

Once all the above was in place it was important to ensure that the Star Zone provided a stimulating and purposeful place of learning ready to respond to the diverse needs of students with emotional and behavioural difficulties. In the Star Zone students are offered a range of learning opportunities. For some students it is important that they are encouraged to work on the curriculum area from which they have been withdrawn. In order to support the staff in the Star Zone, colleagues in subject departments are expected to provide schemes of work and the relevant resources to facilitate this. For other students there is a structured programme of group activities relating to (for example) anger management, assertiveness training and enhancing self-esteem. One of the most difficult elements to juggle was the constant comings and goings of individual students; some of whom were spending much more time in the Star Zone than others. I wanted each of them to feel part of a homogeneous group and in order to achieve this I also included in the curriculum topics that all Star Zone students could contribute to no matter what their age or curriculum level. The kinds of topics we have studied include 'Tourism in Europe', 'A journey through space' and 'The Five Senses'. We play board games, card games and behaviour skills games. Students learn about turn taking, sharing, honesty and a host of other social skills. As a result some of the students made two board games of their own. One was called 'The Star Zone House of Horrors' based on Snakes and Ladders, and the other was based on the Highway Code. As well as the weekly tutorial, staff in the Star Zone keep a record of pupils' work. This provides an on-going record of what the pupil has been working on in the Star Zone, and an assessment and evaluation of the task with recommendations for further work to ensure progress.

PROFESSIONAL DEVELOPMENT

As well as the work with students I am committed to the professional development of colleagues in school. The Star Zone provides staff in school with a range of practical resources that may be borrowed and photocopied on a variety of issues relating to behaviour management. I provide support to newly qualified teachers in their first year of teaching through in-service training sessions, and interns on placement in the school are invited to spend time in the Star Zone as well as having a workshop session on behaviour management. Courses on specific topics are organised using outside speakers that staff can attend: for example, attention deficit hyperactivity disorder, autistic spectrum disorders and bullying in schools. Through this part of my work I am able to maintain and enhance the relationships I have with all the external agencies that support the school on a regular basis. At staff meetings we are continually looking at ways in which we can develop further the work we do to support students. Our next project is to strengthen our links with an EBD special school by buying in the work of an art therapist.

INCLUSIVE EDUCATION

'Schools need effective and well understood arrangements to support teachers and other staff dealing with pupils who cause difficulties' (DfEE 1999). The Star Zone is the way in which one school in Oxfordshire has chosen to support both staff and pupils and deal with the problems of student disaffection through inclusion. Inclusive education means many things to many people. The government believes that the 'education of children with special educational needs is a key challenge for the nation. It is vital to the creation of a fully inclusive society . . . ' (DfEE 1998). Furthermore one of the key themes set out in the Green Paper was to promote 'the inclusion of children with special educational needs within mainstream schooling wherever possible . . . ' (DfEE 1997). The greatest challenge is coming to some kind of consensus within a school community as to what is meant by 'inclusive education'. Inclusion is not a simple concept that relates solely to issues concerned with where a pupil is educated. Ensuring that pupils remain within the mainstream system is important but it cannot be the sole aim of inclusive education. There are too many other considerations to take into account when trying to include pupils with emotional and behavioural difficulties. These include the learning and progress of other pupils and the well-being and stress levels of the teaching staff and other adults. At our school we have agreed that inclusion is a process not a state and the Star Zone is an important part of that process. What we have tried to do in the Star Zone is to ensure that all the issues relating to that process are taken into account when working with students who are vulnerable to exclusion.

In the Star Zone the diversity of all students is valued and they are encouraged to concentrate and develop the talents and skills they have. We are currently looking at fast-tracking a student through GCSE art. Reintegration back into mainstream lessons, therefore, focuses primarily on pupils' strengths and interests in order to ensure success. In the Star Zone we recognise that inclusion is a collective responsibility and we work very closely with groups and agencies not directly concerned with education. As a technology college we are able to develop our links with local businesses to encourage, mentor and reward students. Above all else a definition of inclusion must incorporate notions of respect and dignity. All students and their parents have a right to be treated with respect and have their views taken into account. We have thus come full circle in acknowledging that without good personal relationships inclusion can be elusive.

In the Star Zone we try to empower and enable students to apply themselves to their schoolwork. We try to focus on process and effort, not always on outcomes. We engender positive attitudes and nurture students' emotional well-being. At all times we involve parents in their child's learning. At the end of each day we encourage students to look back, not to focus on what might have gone wrong, but to ask 'what have I done today to make me feel proud?' This may sound too good to be true but I have a firm belief that the success of the Star Zone is due, in no small part, to the faith the school has in me and the staff working in the centre. Equally, the staff in the Star Zone believe in the ability and capacity of the students to succeed. 'Why, sometimes I've believed as many as six impossible things before breakfast' (Lewis Carroll, *Through the Looking Glass*, 1871).

REFERENCES

Bernard, M. (1996) *You Can Do It!* Student Guide. Brighton: Anglo Scholarship Group.

Brighouse, T. & Woods, D. (1999) *How to Improve your School*. London: Routledge.

Canter, L. & Canter, M. (1992) *Assertive Discipline. Positive Behaviour Management for Today's Classroom*. USA: Lee Canter and Associates.

Department for Education and Employment (1997) *Excellence for all Children. Meeting Special Educational Needs*. London: The Stationery Office.

Department for Education and Employment (1998) *Meeting Special Educational Needs. A programme of action*. Sudbury: DfEE Publications Centre.

Department for Education and Employment (1999) *Social Inclusion: Pupil Support*. London: The Stationery Office

Dreikurs, R. and Cassel, P. (1972) *Discipline Without Tears*. USA: Plume.

Fullan, M. (1991) *The New Meaning of Educational Change*. London: Cassell.

Galvin, P. Miller, A. & Nash, J. (1999) *Behaviour and Discipline in Schools*. London: David Fulton.

Gordon, T. (1974) *Teacher Effectiveness Training*. New York: Peter H. Wyden.

Hill, F. and Parsons, L. (2000) *Teamwork in the Management of Emotional and Behavioural Difficulties*. London: David Fulton.

MacGilchrist, B., Myers, K. & Reed, J. (1997) *The Intelligent School.* London: Paul Chapman.

Parsons, L. (1992) *Managing Difficult Behaviour in Mainstream Schools* (unpublished dissertation).

Rogers, W. (1990) *You Know the Fair Rule.* Hawthorn, Victoria, Australia: ACER.

Rogers, W. (1992) *Supporting Teachers in the Workplace.* Queensland: Jacaranda Press.

Rogers, W. (1993) *The Language of Discipline.* Plymouth: Northcote House.

8

The ADHD dilemma: understanding and managing the condition

Lorelei Carpenter

The disorder known as ADHD (Attention Deficit Hyperactivity Disorder) is well known – some would say 'well entrenched' in our schools. Teachers daily, hourly, seek to understand and manage the inattentiveness, distractibility, hyperactivity and impulsiveness symptomatic of ADHD.

Lorelei Carpenter has long researched the issue of ADHD behaviours in schools. In this essay, she goes beyond the label of ADD/ADHD, and its popular misconceptions, to explore the relationship between ADHD and learning and behaviour disorders. The issue of diagnosis, labelling and medication are all discussed. Central to any effective management of ADHD behaviour is a realistic and empathetic understanding of relationship-building between teacher, student and parent(s). Lorelei discusses the crucial nature of relationships in on-going management, support and behaviour change. Managing ADHD is both challenging and stressful and Lorelei argues for a supportive colleague approach.

Students who have been labelled as having attention deficit hyperactivity disorder (ADHD) often represent a conspicuous and somewhat provocative population in most Australian schools. It is estimated that between 2% and 6% of Australian children have the condition (Marshall & Watt, 1999). A significant number of such children have been placed on medication to control their condition. Whether or not we believe that ADHD is a legitimate medical disorder, the reality is that students with the label of ADHD present a challenge to their school and teachers. The challenge is made more difficult by the confusion and uncertainty that continues to surround ADHD despite it being one of the most well researched childhood conditions of our time (Carpenter, 1999). In addition there exists a plethora of conflicting scientific information and populist beliefs associated with the condition. The abundance of information on ADHD is correlated to the reputation of the condition – earned by the end of the 20th century – of being the most frequently diagnosed complaint of childhood (Armstrong, 1996; Baker & McCal, 1996).

The term ADHD has been in use since the late 1980s (American Psychiatric Association, 1987). The medical profession used ADHD to replace other 'labels' such as ADD, hyperactivity, minimal brain dysfunction, minimal brain damage and hyperkinesis. Labels such as these have been used since the early twentieth century to describe a population of students with a diverse range of behavioural and learning difficulties. The characteristics that are most often associated with these labels include inability to focus on tasks, impulsivity and hyperactive behaviour. As well as these, students are marked by their persistent challenging behaviour in spite of the wide range of traditional behaviour management strategies used to control them. Frequently these students are labelled as *uncontrollable*. Consequently, the label has become synonymous with ADHD and visibly positions the condition as being the fault of the student.

As we begin the 21st century controversy and uncertainty continues to be associated with ADHD. Many people still wonder (both silently and aloud) if ADHD is just a label that excuses the wilful behaviour of those children who require firmer discipline. Within the context of education, teachers continue to search for answers about ADHD that will assist them to develop classrooms that are effective learning environments for students such as these. The most frequently asked questions that relate to ADHD refer to the controversy inherent in ADHD. Such questions represent public sentiment and teachers' uncertainty and doubts related to the condition. These include questions about the authenticity of ADHD as a medical disorder, the necessity for using medication to control the condition and the type of classroom strategies that can be effectively used with children labelled with ADHD.

In this chapter I examine how these questions affect teachers by discussing the challenging issues influencing the questions. In addition, I discuss ways in which teachers can manage children who have ADHD. The position I take is that despite the populist notion that we live in a simplistic world the fact is that life in Western society is complex. Thus when considering child behaviour and how to manage it we cannot expect to have quick fix solutions that simply aim at 'curing' the child. Instead we need to view what we consider to be a child's inappropriate behaviour within the context of a complex society. Such a society is challenged by economic stresses, changes to family life and claims on time that interfere with raising children and influence the educational environment.

An indication of the conundrum of ADHD is represented in the popular press by what appears to be a biased view against ADHD. For example, Wallis (1994) wrote in *Time Weekly Magazine* of the unrest and uncertainty of ADHD as a medical condition. She argued that the inaccuracy of ADHD diagnosis was caused by the lack of objective methods of assessment and that 'in the absence of any biological test, diagnosing ADHD is a rather inexact proposition' (p 35). She represented the growing cynicism about ADHD by stating that 'doctors say huge numbers of kids and adults have attention deficit disorder . . . is it for real?' (p 31).

Similarly the numerous newspaper articles in the Australian press underscore the emotion and confusion caused by the uncertainty over ADHD. In Queensland, the front page of *The Sunday Mail* carried the caption 'Drug Shame – Kids who queue to be sedated' (Lawrence, 1998, p 1). The accompanying full-page photo showed a line of primary school children reportedly waiting to be given their medication at school. The full report 'Row over virus of the 90's' (Lawrence, 1998, p 4) claimed that some doctors believed ADHD was being over diagnosed, with the label being given to any children who were not well behaved. The same article interviewed doctors who believed there was an under diagnosis of the condition particularly in girls. A week later the same newspaper questioned the purpose of medicating children at pre-school in articles such as 'Learning the sedate way of life' (Sweetman 1998, p 10) and 'Zombie heartbreak' (Griffith, 1998, p 14). These articles reported on the heartbreak teachers experience having to administer medication to children under directions from doctors and parents. Further emotive headlines continue to fuel the debate about ADHD. These include 'Mind drugs are hurting normal children' (Reardon, 1999, p 5), and 'Doctors dope unruly tots' (Mickleburgh, 2000, p 6).

WHAT IS ADHD?

The contradictory views of medical professionals who have worked extensively in the field of ADHD indicate the confusion and inaccuracy of the term ADHD. For example, Gordon Serfontein (1990), a paediatric neurologist who claims to have worked with over eight thousand ADHD children, defines ADHD as mainly a disorder, present in behaviour such as significant problems with attention and concentration.

Conversely, Russel Barkley (1981,1996), a professor of psychiatry who has researched ADHD for more than 20 years, describes ADHD as a deficit in inhibiting behaviour rather than a deficit in attention. Barkley argues that the label of ADHD is not really appropriate because the child does not have a deficit of attention but rather a lack of self-control. He argues that the label 'developmental disorder of self-control' (1995, p 53) is more appropriate. According to Barkley (1997) ADHD is a disorder that results from a failure to control and inhibit thoughts and impulses that influence behaviour. In other words it is characterised by a lack of self-control that impairs the brain's ability to inhibit behaviour once it has begun. The inability to self-control and inhibit behaviour can be observed in the child's inattentiveness or in their hyperactive and impulsive behaviour. It is also characterised by the child's inability to switch attention from one task to another when required to do so.

Since 1994 ADHD has been recognised by the American Psychiatric Association as falling into three distinct diagnostic categories. These include ADHD, primarily inattentive (IA); ADHD, primarily hyperactive (HI); and ADHD combined type. The latter 'typing' combines symptoms from the subtypes of HI and IA. Although some medical professionals use these labels there are others who will use the generic term of ADHD or ADD. The variety of labels that has been used over time contributes to the confusion surrounding the condition. With each new label there is a new set of similar yet slightly different characteristics. In short, ADHD has been an ill-defined condition.

The effect of such diverse professional views and labels is that frequently many people become cynical about the validity of ADHD. Thus they refuse to acknowledge that in some cases the condition genuinely exists. The other problem, which is the greatest one facing ADHD, is accepting the legitimate nature of such a 'condition'. There are a percentage of children who need to be recognised as having ADHD and are therefore in need of support and help from medical professionals, teachers and parents to help them negotiate their way through life.

The uncertainty surrounding ADHD is increased by the recognition that it does not often occur alone. There are other conditions that occur along with ADHD. For example, ADHD is frequently associated with learning disabilities, conduct disorder and social skills deficits (Anastopolous, DuPaul & Barkley, 1991; Stanford & Hynd, 1994). Likewise, children with Asperger's syndrome and autism will often display ADHD-like behaviour. In some cases the only condition being treated is ADHD, with the other conditions being ignored and left untreated. For example, following their research Lahey *et al* (1987) claim that approximately half of the children diagnosed with ADHD would also qualify for diagnosis of another disorder. As well it is possible that the diagnosis could be incorrect. It is argued that children with childhood anxiety often exhibit very similar behaviour to children with ADHD (Halperin *et al*, 1993; Simeon *et al*, 1994). Therefore it becomes difficult to distinguish one condition from the other. Here the problem is that a misdiagnosis could result in inappropriate and ineffective treatment.

Why does this occur? The problem may be one of having inaccurate diagnostic tools that allow for an objective decision to be made. ADHD and other associated conditions are behavioural problems. As such they are identified by using checklists, questionnaires, anecdotal information and observations. All of these are measures that are influenced by subjective interpretations, definitions and personal values. To date there has been a lack of acceptable objective measures to use when diagnosing many of these conditions. It could be assumed that the decision to label a child with a certain condition might differ according to the personal interpretation of what each diagnostic criteria means. Another problem could be that the person making the diagnosis has expertise in identifying one condition but not others.

Hence a number of other conditions may be overlooked or mistakenly labelled as ADHD. The child is often labelled as ADHD and the most frequently assigned treatment, medication, is prescribed. In this case other conditions or the true condition remain untreated. This causes further doubt as to whether or not ADHD really exists because the prescribed treatment may not be effective.

ADHD AND OTHER BEHAVIOUR DISORDERS

Along with ADHD, the behavioural disorders of conduct disorder (CD) and oppositional defiant disorder (ODD) are becoming common diagnoses made in

Australia. Once again the frequency of the diagnosis increases with the amount of knowledge and expertise that medical professionals have, the familiarity of the term with parents and the pressure that parents, teachers and others may be exerting on professionals for them to provide labels. The reported incidence rate of these disorders varies greatly between 4% and 16% because of factors that include different definitions that describe the condition (Marshall & Watt, 1999).

Oppositional defiant disorder (ODD) most often occurs in children below the age of ten. ODD occurs in 3–4% of children and causes difficulties at home, school and with peers. It is characterised by argumentativeness, disobedience, stubbornness, negativity and provocation of others. These children would formerly have been called *defiant, stubborn, strong willed* or *determined*. However, these characteristics have now been 'pathologised' and considered aberrant enough to receive a medical label. Conduct disorder (CD) is a more severe behavioural disorder whose incidence rate increases as children reach adolescence. CD is a persistent pattern of misbehaviour that includes violating the rights of others and the moral codes of society through lying, stealing, physical aggression and vandalism (Eddy, 1996).

It is estimated that at least one quarter of children with these behavioural disorders will also have ADHD. Although CD and ODD are beginning to receive increased recognition many children are labelled as ADHD and other conditions are frequently not identified. Both CD and ODD require parent training as well as community based intervention. Nevertheless, the chosen method of treatment is often medication which is prescribed for the ADHD symptoms that frequently occur with these disorders.

Here the problem is that the dimension of a severe behavioural disorder is added to ADHD. This can lead to confusion when an attempt is made to compare one ADHD child with another. There may be very little similarity between the two children. Thus the faulty conclusion could be reached that the condition does not exist in the child whose behaviour appears to be less severe.

CONTROVERSY AND CONFUSION OVER ADHD

The politics of labelling

The growing number of labels, the uncertainty of what they mean and the lack of a simple means of managing these conditions add to the confusion and controversy over conditions such as ADHD. People, both professional and non-professional, have popularised the medically oriented labels of 'ADHD' and 'hyperactive' by using them as common terms for the behaviour of those children who formerly may have been called *hard to handle*.

Since the middle of the 20th century there has been an ironic development in relation to childhood behaviour. A strong sense of what is normal behaviour developed particularly in the last half of the 20th century. At the same time the medical profession began developing a list of childhood conditions that presently number over 200. These are regularly added to and are used to label those children whose behaviour falls outside the accepted mythical normal behaviour. In many cases these labels are invaluable in providing children with the support and treatment that they require to function socially. However, it is often the case that the child with ADHD is treated but not supported. Despite research (Cantwell, 1996; DuPaul & Barkley, 1990; Weiss, 1996; Wender, 1995) that has repeatedly stressed the importance of a combination of medication, behaviour modification, counselling, social skills training and family therapy, the reality is that medication remains the most popular single choice of treatment.

In contemporary Western society that is both 'time poor' and 'patience poor' the normal markers of a *good* child are restraint, control, responsibility and dependability. Consequently the group of behaviours such as *bold, naughty, cheeky, insolent* and *defiant* are frequently replaced by the label *ADHD*. In particular these behaviours attract this label if they appear to be unmanageable and uncontrollable. Within another society that has more time and patience such exuberant and strong-minded behaviour may be encouraged and nurtured as normal manifestations of childhood. In our society the child's behaviour comes under medical management via the use of medication. In some cases the 'condition' the child may be suffering from is *childhood*. A preferred treatment would be adult support and some freedom for the child to experiment with behaviours in order to determine which are best suited for life. However, the growing list of labels invites many questions. For example, does the normal child exist or has normalcy become a myth? Who benefits from this extensive list of complaints? Are we becoming a society that accepts difference only if it can be chemically controlled and shaped to suit the construct of normalcy?

The challenge of medication

Many teachers experience a growing concern that ADHD is reaching epidemic proportions because an increasing number of children from pre-school to secondary school have the label. This concern is heightened by the correspond-ing rise in the use of medication such as Methylphenidate, commonly known as Ritalin, Dexamphetamine or a combination of these and other medications to control the condition. The use of medication to manage ADHD is one of the most controversial and debated areas associated with the condition. The debate is generated mostly by the belief that the child's behaviour will be controlled and changed through taking the prescribed drugs. However, many teachers continue to discover that while the medication may decrease inappropriate behaviour in some children there is often no corresponding increase in appropriate behaviour. Not all children respond positively to taking medication. For example, Brown (2000) estimates that between 10% and 30% of students may not respond to medication. Thus, classes continue to be disrupted in spite of certain students (with ADHD) being medicated.

One of the problems of using medication is that we live in a society where contradictions abound regarding the use of drugs. On the one hand there is widespread use of prescription drugs, tobacco, alcohol and leisure drugs. Yet, there is public outcry at the use of drugs for children and adolescents. In the case of ADHD newspapers often use headlines that condemn parents who use medication to manage their child's ADHD. For example, 'Misuse common, says doctor' (Lawrence, 1998, p 14) reports that doctors are seeing a small percentage of parents who ask for a diagnosis of ADHD so they can claim a fortnightly carers pension. In some doctors' opinion the children are simply difficult to handle and do not have 'the condition'. Occasionally there are articles such as those reported in the *Sun Herald* that attempt to provide a balanced view on the drug conundrum. Yet it seems captions such as 'Mummy's little helper' (Shine, 2001, p 29) 'Toddlers given Prozac' (Shine, 2001, p 7) and 'The drugs we use to control our kids' (Shine, 2001, p 33) clearly indicate an underlying message of condemnation of parents who medicate their children. Interestingly, an article in the *Sydney Morning Herald* (Riley, 2001) bearing the headline 'Kiddie cocaine: It's the drug of the new generation?' signals the ADHD conundrum. The article reports a case in New York State in which a father was threatened with having his son removed from his care because he refused to give him Ritalin that had been prescribed to help overcome his learning problems. The father was concerned because he had observed his effervescent and energetic son change to being timid and reserved since taking the medication. The same article reported on a study at the University of California that has found a connection between using Ritalin in childhood and later cocaine addiction.

The complexity of 'post-modern' life becomes apparent when we consider this ambiguous stance taken when an attempt is made to solve the question of how best to raise children today. Articles such as the above emphasise the dilemma that both parents and teachers face regarding the use of drugs with children. Most education systems demand that parents 'do something' if a child is considered uncontrollable. Yet, if parents, particularly mothers, succumb to allowing their child to be medicated they are severely criticised and condemned for making their child 'drug-dependant'. On the other hand they are labelled as bad parents if they are considered unable to manage their child's behaviour by refusing to administer the treatment prescribed by society. Teachers face a similar dilemma. The question of whether or not children with ADHD should be medicated adds further to the stresses that seem to grow daily in classrooms. If teachers approve of medicating students to manage behaviour then they are seen to condone 'drug-taking behaviour'. Alternatively if teachers actively discourage parents from resorting to giving their child medication then they face the possibility of having a highly disruptive student in a situation that is already stressful and demanding.

Hence the public uncertainty and confusion over ADHD is reflected in the dilemma that parents and teachers experience in managing the condition. Numerous questions exist regarding the condition yet few answers are provided regarding the reality of what to do with children who are diagnosed with ADHD.

Moreover clear messages are given regarding what is considered appropriate and inappropriate behaviour. Yet on the other hand no such clarity exists when it comes to managing what is considered to be the inappropriate behaviour of conditions such as ADHD. The search for an answer reflects our desire to live simply in an increasingly complex society. As well the search for a simple means of treating the child with ADHD reflects society's need to treat the 'product of society' rather than to examine itself to discover how that 'product' originated. Yet there is no simple way of treating ADHD. It is a complex condition that occurs in a complex society. Furthermore, children are most often treated as the perpetrators and not the victims of such a society. Each child requires treatment to suit their unique situation and needs.

STRATEGIES

Managing students who show difficult behaviour is a risky business. The risk occurs in developing and trying new strategies that may not be successful. Yet working with challenging students brings its rewards when they begin to cope effectively, if only for a short time. Regardless of the accuracy of the label that is used to identify students, the fact is that classrooms contain students whose behaviour is very difficult to handle. What follows are suggestions for managing and supporting those students who have been labelled as having ADHD or who display the type of behaviour that could be identified as ADHD. When dealing with students such as these it is often useful to remember that while a management strategy may work for a short time it may not continue to be successful. Therefore it is preferable to have a number of strategies that can be discarded once they become ineffective and recycled at a later time. It is useful to remember that all children are individuals. Hence, a strategy that is effective for one student may not necessarily suit another student.

Parent-teacher relationship

Get to know the ADHD child's parents; it is often the case that they can be your strongest supporters. Most parents are able to empathise with teachers regarding the difficulty of coping with their child. Frequently parents have become experts regarding their child's condition because they have lived with their child's ADHD for many years and have had to overcome many challenges. It is often the case that they have punished and scolded their ADHD child for their inappropriate behaviour since they began to walk and talk. Parents may have developed an excellent understanding of their child, and what works best for them. The teacher, too, may have discovered other strategies that work successfully with the student. Both teacher and parents can share their expertise on how to manage and support the child in various situations. Moreover, both the teacher and the parents may have the same goal of 'surviving' the child's

ADHD while doing what is best for the child. Regular contact between the teacher and the student's parents is, therefore, an important aspect of any management approach.

When dealing with parents, teachers need to remember that it is often the case they have spent many years being told by other people that they are 'bad' parents (Carpenter, 1999). Parents of all children who have difficulties need respectful and considerate support from schools. Society has clearly defined expectations of how a child must behave in order for the parents to be acknowledged as 'good' parents. Ironically it has few successful methods of teaching parents how to be 'good'. Most parents try, to the best of their ability, to raise their children according to the requirements of society. Yet many parents of ADHD children have experienced the stigma and the social isolation of having a child who is labelled as uncontrollable. In some cases parents may require training and support from the school to successfully manage the difficult behaviour of their child. One of the essentials of a successful behaviour programme is that it has some continuity at home and at school.

Student-teacher relationship

The first step in dealing with any student who may appear to be behaving inappropriately is to develop a friendly relationship with that child. This can often be difficult because ADHD students tend to project an image of being tough, insensitive, belligerent, argumentative and unlikable. However, such a facade often hides their sensitivity, need for friendship, desire to belong and their fear that the label of 'naughty' and 'bad' means they are undeserving of acceptance. The majority of children begin school with the expectation that they will be liked and will be part of a group. Many children have the necessary social skills and behaviours that allow this to occur. Yet some children are genuinely unable to mix socially with their peers because of their behaviour. As well, some students repeatedly make the wrong decisions when they are trying to do the right thing. As a result, over time, with repeated failures to socialise and to be accepted by their teacher, they can appear to be making few attempts to help this happen.

Many teachers will argue that students who behave inappropriately have done so through their own choice and therefore deserve the punishment, isolation and marginalisation that most of them experience. In some cases this is true. Often their behaviour appears to be deliberately chosen. Many students with ADHD may abandon trying to behave appropriately because the cost of repeated failure becomes too painful. It is often the case that since early childhood, students have found that being the class clown, the one with the loudest voice or the argumentative one may provides them with more attention and a sense of belonging than if they attempted to sit quietly and remain unnoticed.

The best way to develop a relationship is by listening to and talking with the student. Find a quiet time when you can have a conversation together. Talk about things that have nothing to do with the student's behaviour. Discover their interests particularly those outside school. Talk to this student with genuine interest; demonstrating you want to find out something about them. Frequently you will be pleasantly surprised to find that you discover a sensitive, likeable and knowledgeable person who has many worthwhile things to share with you. What seems to be the case with many students with ADHD is that they do well with a lot of one-on-one attention as it seems to stimulate them so that they can stay on the task at hand.

Students with ADHD can often relate better to older students or adults. Hence it is useful to pair them with someone who can be their mentor or guide. Although we often think that children must be taught to socialise with their own age group, with some children this is not possible. It is often far better to stop forcing the ADHD student to be friendly with their own age group as they often experience difficulty coping with their peers. It is better for a student to have at least one friend, regardless of their age, than to have no friends at all. Moreover ADHD students will often be more inclined to model themselves after someone older and to be influenced by them.

The need for support

Teaching a student with ADHD can be confronting, challenging and stressful. Teachers of ADHD students frequently question whether they are successful in their role and whether they should continue teaching. Therefore teachers need a colleague with whom they can debrief. Debriefing is best done in private, preferably not in the staff room, as discussing a student (by name) in front of other people may lead to that student being labelled and developing a reputation which is often difficult to reverse.

Most students do not do well when they are isolated, sent to the head teacher's office or kept apart from their peers. On the other hand it is frequently necessary to remove an ADHD student from a classroom (for periodic time-out) to provide the teacher, other students and the ADHD student with some 'respite'. This can be done in a positive rather than a negative manner. For example, arrange with a colleague to send the student to their class to be a helper or tutor for a set time each day or several days a week. Many students with ADHD do well when they are given responsibility to tutor students in younger grades. In particular ADHD students have an excellent understanding of what is considered good behaviour because they have so often been told by others how they are expected to behave. Although they may be unable to display good behaviour they know what to expect from others.

Responsive schools that successfully work with students with ADHD do so by using a team approach. It is difficult for a classroom teacher to be solely responsible for implementing a management programme. The teacher requires support in the form of maximum cooperation from the whole school. This takes the form of other staff members understanding the nature of the management programme and ensuring the continuity of the programme by reinforcing it in a similar manner to the class teacher. This means that staff will becomes familiar with the individual needs of the student with ADHD and the way in which those needs can best be met.

Classroom environment

The design of classrooms and schools and the way they are managed frequently *set students up* to misbehave. For example, open area classrooms and double classrooms are unsuitable for those students who have a low tolerance to noise and movement. Classrooms that use strategies of co-operative learning are also often unsuitable for many students. This is because desk grouping that encourages student interaction is often too distracting for students with ADHD. Such students generally experience difficulty in controlling their behaviour in a highly stimulating environment designed for social interaction. Oftentimes they will begin to talk loudly, move around the room and behave inappropriately.

Traditional classrooms that arrange desks in rows seem most suited to students who present with ADHD behaviours, because their communication and movement is more controlled and restricted. Classrooms such as these may appear to be boring and uninteresting as well as too restrictive and quiet for some students to work in. However, this type of safe and structured environment may actually have the effect of encouraging some ADHD students to work productively. There are fewer interruptions and distractions and students have a clear idea of the limits that they are to work within.

Working with aspects of ADHD

The difficulty that some ADHD students experience in controlling their emotions or separating out their emotion from the event often compounds the difficulty of managing these students. Thus a student with ADHD may become highly emotional over something that other students would have less of a reaction to. ADHD students may appear to be angrier, sadder or more excited and may be considered extremely emotional and unable to hide the extremes of their emotion. In other words they experience more highs and lows than many other students do. This is where the term 'hyperactive' is often used to describe an ADHD child who is displaying some exaggerated emotion. Behaviour such as this can be difficult and wearing for a classroom teacher who is expected to cope with the emotions of all the students as well as her own reaction to these. It is useful to provide these students with the opportunity to let off steam and to deal more constructively with their emotions. Often it is the case that once a student has appropriately released high levels of emotional arousal they will be much calmer.

Students with ADHD have problems with self-direction. Their system of internalised self-speech that helps to control and order behaviour, solve problems and to remind them of rules is absent or slow to develop (Barkley,

1995). This means that they are unable to engage in private self-talk such as 'That won't work. I've tried it before', 'The last time I did that I was in trouble', 'I can't do that. It's against the rules'. Some ADHD students need to be taught how to engage in using a system of internal language so that they can ask themselves questions and talk their way through a problem. Visual prompts can be taught to them and placed in a location such as on their desk to act as reminders of the questions they need to ask themselves. For example, 'I have to put up my hand to ask a question', 'I need to stay in my seat after I've finished my work', 'I take out a book to read when I have nothing to do', 'Is what I'm doing against the rules?', 'What else can I do?'

Students with ADHD usually experience the same type of organisational difficulty in relation to their environment. These students often appear to be untidy and frequently have difficulty in working on oral and written presentations. Despite their attempts at being organised they seem unable to begin an assignment or project and once begun they are usually lost or forget what to do. In this case students require simple instructions on how to organise themselves and how to remain organised. The skills and knowledge of organised behaviour that most other students are able to develop through observation and incidental learning are seldom learnt by ADHD students. In particular they will often require repeated, simple, step-by-step instructions on how to begin, maintain and complete tasks.

Related to this problem of self-direction is the ADHD student's difficulty in remembering the goals of a task and anticipating the consequences of their actions. What students do in the present is seldom influenced by their memory of the consequences of similar actions in the past, or of the anticipated consequences of their actions in the future. The student with ADHD will benefit from being taught strategies such as 'Stop Think Do' (Petersen & Gannoni, 1992) which will assist the student to be less impulsive and to be more thoughtful when choosing behaviour.

Whatever skills are taught to students with ADHD they will require constant reinforcement. This is because many ADHD children have difficulty applying what has been learnt in prior situations to new situations. It is as though what has been learnt repeatedly in the past makes little difference to the present behaviour. Thus many ADHD students seem to habitually engage in the same behaviour that results in the same consequences without appearing to learn from their past mistakes. This represents a significant time waster as each problem is approached as if there is no prior learning. It is equally frustrating for the ADHD student as it is for the teacher. Therefore it is important to use checklists, notes, and any type of reminders that will act as scaffolds to support the student in their attempts to behave appropriately.

Some teachers may believe that it is a waste of time putting these strategies in place. However, the time that is invested initially will be more than compensated for, as it will save the teacher's time during the year. As well it may prevent them from succumbing to undue stress.

CONCLUSION

The uncertainty regarding the condition of ADHD is one of the many challenges that teachers are required to confront when working with students who have difficult behaviour. The ADHD student, more than most students, needs adults who can use their time and patience to persevere, support, encourage and believe in them. Students with ADHD often have the ability to use their behaviours in many fields that will enable them to achieve success. Many will go on to adulthood and enjoy success in roles that require and reward their unique characteristics. Others may be unable to utilise their skills and energy in a positive way. Moreover, despite the frustration that some students can present, working with them can be immensely rewarding.

The debate regarding the legitimacy and the accuracy of the ADHD condition will continue until such time as there is an accurate, objective means of proving whether or not the condition exists and who has the condition. However, if we acknowledge that there are some students who have a genuine behavioural disability then it is our responsibility to provide them with the same consideration, respect, support and modifications that are provided in response to the unique needs of those students who have other disabilities.

REFERENCES

American Psychiatric Association (1987) *Diagnostic and statistical manual of mental disorders* (3rd edn.). Washington, DC: Author.

Anastopoulos, A., DuPaul, G., & Barkley, R. (1991) Stimulant medication and parent training therapies for attention deficit-hyperactivity disorder. *Journal of Learning Disabilities*, 24, 210–217.

Armstrong, T. (1996) ADD: Does it really exist? *Phi Delta Kappan,* 77(6), 424–428.

Baker, D., & McCal, M. (1995). Parenting stress in parents of children with attention-deficit hyperactivity disorder and parents of children with learning disabilities. *Journal of Child and Family Studies*, 4(1), 57–68.

Barkley, R. (1981) *Hyperactive children: Handbook for diagnosis and treatment*. New York: Guilford Press.

Barkley, R. (1995) *Taking charge of ADHD: The complete authoritative guide for parents*. New York: Guilford Press.

Barkley, R. (1996) Attention-deficit hyperactivity disorder. In E. Mash & R. Barkley (eds.) *Child psychopathology,* (pp 63–112). New York: Guilford Press.

Barkley, R. (1997) Behavioural inhibition, sustained attention, and executive functions: Constructing a unifying theory of ADHD. *Psychological Bulletin*, 121(1), 65–94.

Brown, M. (2000) Diagnosis and treatment of children and adolescents with attention-deficit/hyperactivity disorder. *Journal of Counselling and Development*, 78(2), 195–203.

Cantwell, D. (1996) Attention deficit disorder: A review of the past 10 years. *American Academy of Child and Adolescent Psychiatry*, 35, 978–987.

Carpenter, L. (1999) The effect of a child's attention deficit hyperactivity disorder on a mother: The hidden disability of motherhood. Unpublished doctoral dissertation, Griffith University, Brisbane, Australia.

Cherkes-Julkowski, M., Sharp, S. & Stolzenberg, J. (1997) *Rethinking attention deficit disorders*. Cambridge, MA: Brookline Books.

DuPaul, G., & Barkley, R. (1990) Medication therapy. In R. Barkley (ed.), *Attention-deficit hyperactivity disorder: A handbook for diagnosis and treatment* (pp 573–612). New York: Guilford Press.

Eddy, J. (1996) *Conduct disorders: The latest assessment and treatment strategies*. Kansas City, MO: Compact Clinicals.

Griffith, C. (1998, March,1) Zombie heartbreak. *The Sunday Mail* p 14.

Halperin, J., Newcorn, J., Matier, K. & Sharma, V. (1993) Discriminant validity of attention deficit hyperactivity disorder. *Journal of the American Academy of Child & Adolescent Psychiatry,* 32(5), 1038–1043.

Lahey, B., Schaughency, E., Hynd, G., Carlson, C., & Nieves, N. (1987). Attention deficit disorder with and without hyperactivity: Comparison of behavioural characteristics of clinic referred children. *Journal of the American Academy of Child and Adolescent Psychiatry*, 26, 718–723.

Lawrence, K. (1998, February, 22). Drug shame – Kids who queue to be sedated. *The Sunday Mail* p 1.

(1998, February, 22) Row over virus of the 90's. *The Sunday Mail* p 4.

(1998, March, 1) Misuse common says doctor. *The Sunday Mail* p 14.

Mickelburgh, R. (2000, April, 30) Doctors dope unruly tots. *The Sunday Mail* p 6.

Marshall, J. & Watt, P. (1999) *Child behaviour problems: A literature review of the size and nature of the problem*. Perth, WA: Interagency Committee on Children's Futures.

Petersen, L. & Gannoni, A. (1992) *Teacher's manual for training social skills while managing student behaviour*. Hawthorn, Vic: ACER.

Reardon, D. (1999, February, 6) Mind drugs are hurting normal children. *Sydney Morning Herald* p 5.

Riley, M. (2001, February, 21) Kiddie cocaine: It's the drug of the new generation. *Sydney Morning Herald* p 1.

Serfontein, G. (1990) *The hidden handicap: How to help children who suffer from dyslexia, hyperactivity and learning difficulties*. Sydney, Australia: Simon & Schuster.

Shine, K. (2001, February, 18) Mummy's little helper. *Sun Herald* p 29.

(2001, February, 18) The drugs we use to control our kids. *Sun Herald* p 33.

(2001, February, 18) Toddlers given Prozac. *Sun Herald* p 7.

Simeon, J., Knott, V., Dubois, C., & Wiggins, D. (1994) Buspirone therapy of mixed anxiety disorders in childhood and adolescence: A pilot study.

Journal of Child & Adolescent Psychopharmacology, 4(3), 159–170.

Sweetman, T. (1998, March, 1) Learning the sedate way of life. *The Sunday Mail* p 10.

Wallis, C. (1994, September 5) Life in overdrive. *Time Weekly Magazine,* 36, 31–42.

Weiss, G. (1996). Attention deficit hyperactivity disorder. In M. Lewis (ed.) *Child and adolescent psychiatry: A comprehensive textbook* (pp 544–563). Baltimore: Williams & Wilkins.

Wender, P. (1995). *Attention-deficit hyperactivity disorder in adults.* New York: Oxford University Press.

9

Technology and behaviour management: identifying strategic intents – understanding and creating new environments

Dr Glenn Finger

For many teachers, technology (in the form of computers, word processing and the ubiquitous Internet) is an inevitable challenge as much as it is a necessity. Glenn Finger has had many years experience in teacher education and emergent technology. Today's children have grown up with and are often quite comfortable with computers and the Internet and CD Roms, etc.; they easily see the connectedness to their education and schooling. Glenn argues that schools – and teachers – are somewhat resistant to ideas, approaches and skills cognate with new and emergent technologies. He develops a paradigm of educational thinking that seeks to come to terms with the new environment of computer-based technologies. Of particular interest and focus is how much technology affects the nature of what Glenn terms the 'collegial classroom' and the implications this has for management, discipline and co-operative learning.

START...PROGRAMS, DOCUMENTS, SETTINGS, FIND, HELP, RUN...

In the opening graphics to the report on *National Educational Technology Standards for Students* (ISTE, 2000), the International Society for Technology in Education (ISTE) provocatively states:

> *'Ready or not...*
> *The World is Different*
> *Kids are different...*
> *Learning is different...*
> *And Teaching Must Be Different, too.'* (ISTE, 2000, pp 1–2)

The ISTE quote highlights the orientation of this chapter, which starts from the premise that 'the world is different' and that 'kids are different'. Given a brief to provoke and share ideas about the new and emerging technologies and their implications for school leadership and behaviour management, I've attempted to capture some of the excitement of the new environments provided by computers and the Internet. Hence this initial section is headed *Start* using terminology consistent with the options found on the *Task Bar* of your computer screen: *Programs, Documents, Settings, Find, Help,* and *Run.* In this chapter, school leaders are urged to consider four strategic intents which are required in developing their strategic technology and behaviour *programs* and *documents* in their diverse *settings,* and to assist in providing some *help* to *run* those programs. *Bookmarks* identify those four strategic intents – *Understanding new environments, Creating new environments, Identifying teachers' roles* and *Meeting technology-related needs. Screens* provide images for school leaders to assist them in navigating their way to take advantage of the potential which the new and emerging technologies hold for increasing student motivation, enhancing student engagement and connecting with students to improve behaviour management.

In conceptualising the organisation of this chapter, I considered adopting the usual writing planning process of starting with an introduction, ending with a conclusion and organising key ideas and content in the normal way. However, I was reminded of a book about computers and writing which I critically reviewed for use by my University students. The book outlined new ways of publishing work through word processing and desktop publishing. This all sounded very exciting as it discussed strategies for making the presentation of students' work more interesting through incorporating design features. As I read the book, which presented great ideas, there was something missing. The presentation of that book itself did not model those new ideas. Traditional fonts were used, no graphics were inserted, the layout seemed designed to assist insomniacs rather than inspire teachers, and the references to useful websites indicated that there was little sense in including these as they changed so often. Reading the book was similar to swimming without getting wet, like someone searching for a website without connecting to the Internet, and as Lewis Carroll's Alice thought, 'What use is a book without pictures or conversations?' What follows is an attempt to provide some of those pictures and provoke some of those conversations.

BOOKMARK 1: UNDERSTANDING NEW ENVIRONMENTS... HIT 'ENTER'

> 'The illiterate of the 21st century will not be those who cannot read and write, but those who cannot learn, unlearn, and relearn.' – Alvin Toffler

The first bookmark flags the need for us to enter the new and different worlds in which children are immersed. Students in schools today have been immersed in a technological world substantially different from that of those born more than a decade or so ago. For example, Barlow (in Tunbridge, 1996) refers to two categories as 'natives' and 'immigrants'.

" . . .generally speaking, if you're over 25, you're an immigrant. If you're under 25 you're closer to being a native, in terms of understanding what it [the internet and the IT world generally] is and having a real basic sense of it.' (Barlow in Tunbridge, 1996)

Similarly, Williams and McKeown (1996) refer to tourists, immigrants and natives when they describe 'Teachers' experiences of the Internet are akin to those of people who become involved in a different country' and subsequently, as tourists or immigrants, teachers adopt a conventional information model of the Internet. Mackay (1997) categorised three generations of Australians as the Lucky Generation, the Baby Boomers and the Options Generation and provided a comparison of their attitudes and beliefs, values and lifestyles. Interestingly, Mackay argues that those belonging to the Options Generation (born during the last 25 years) are better equipped to deal with the changes evident in our post-modern society characterised by rapid, dynamic technological developments. A phenomenon referred to as the 'teaching inversion' is being identified, whereby we:

'. . .currently have the situation where a significant proportion of the young have a greater knowledge of a major domain of learning than their teachers. We have a "Net" generation with an IT competence that generally exceeds that of their teachers and who can teach the adults how to use the new technology.' (Lee, 1998, p 38)

Lee argues that while it would be very easy to dismiss the phenomenon of the 'teaching inversion', today's students are likely to find existing schooling irrelevant and suggests strongly that schools need to audit student competence and to capitalise on the educational potential young students have by providing them 'with a networked learning environment that enables all of them to acquire an education befitting the Information Age' (Lee, 1998, p 41). According to Lee (1999, p 28), the signs point strongly to a new global education system which challenges traditional schooling.

'While the "school" system remains locked in the Industrial Age, and continues to provide primarily an Industrial Age education, the new "Net" education system would appear to be going a long way towards preparing the young to thrive in a knowledge-based society.' (Lee, 1999, p 28)

Various writers (e.g. Mumtaz, 2000) have alerted us to the 'growing gap between children's experience of computers in their two environments of home and school' (p 347). The rich technological environments many children are immersed in at home has been highlighted by Lloyd (1999, p 48) who reported that Logistix Kids (Australia's first consultancy dedicated to the children's market) conducts monthly Kids Monitor surveys and in June 1999 completed a study entitled *The Secret World of the Kid's Bedroom* involving interviews with 400 children in Sydney aged between eight and 13. The study revealed that children consider their bedrooms to be 'high-tech entertainment havens'. The study reported that TV sets, video recorders, computers and CD players are now considered 'normal' bedroom furniture with some children's bedrooms having their own fax machines. Forget Elizabeth Taylor, Lauren Bacall and Marilyn Monroe, and forget the more contemporary megastars Madonna, Nicole Kidman, and Julia Roberts, the highest grossing female entertainer of all time is Lara Croft. If you're either a head teacher or a class teacher unfamiliar with the new multimedia gaming environments of children and youth, you're probably asking, Lara who? Despite not being a real person, Lara Croft was the main character in the *Tomb Raider* suite of games which has grossed more than *Titanic*. Again, I'd guess that most adults are familiar with Kate Winslet and Leonardo Di Caprio, but how many are familiar with Lara Croft and *Tomb Raider*?

Search **Screen 1: 'inside their worlds'**

The gap between legitimised, valued school activity and home 'stuff' was well illustrated in a supervisory visit I undertook to a primary school to liaise with the student teachers undertaking their practicum. After entering a Year 7 classroom, I observed children settling into silent reading. Most received their confirmations through nods and approving glances from the teacher and the student teacher. As the adult eyes scanned across the classroom, two boys suspiciously shuffled magazines under their desks. All three adults moved over closer. The magazines were not from the library. The student teacher asked assertively, 'What are those magazines doing here at school?' The supervising teacher looked at me somewhat embarrassed, as she seemed to feel that her behaviour management was tarnished because these two boys weren't reading suitable material.

I noticed that they were personal computer (PC) games magazines and, after trying to settle the anxiety of the student teacher and the teacher, I asked their permission to have a look at the magazines as, 'I'm interested in new technologies and this sort of stuff'. The discussion with these two students provided me with a rich insight into the latest developments in PC games, the innovative strategies being employed by Sega, Nintendo, Sony and Microsoft. After several questions to start the conversation, these students discussed complex concepts such as the games' developers, publishers, distributors, system requirements such as 'You need a minimum of Windows 98, Intel Pentium 3 running at 650 megs but 1 Gig would be great ... it's multiplayer, it has obscure objectives but I like how its future's oriented, sometimes it irritates me how...'

They both went on to describe Microsoft's plans for the Xbox, and why they didn't think that Sega's Dreamcast would be as successful a platform as Sega was hoping. They not only showed that they could make meaning from the text but were critical text analysts. More importantly, the scene had changed from defensive students feeling marginalised within the classroom to students willing to share their knowledge and critiques.

Our conversation ended by them promising to email me some additional information and some useful websites for my work at University.

In a recent issue of *PC Powerplay* (Norton-Smith, May 2001), the real time strategy (RTS) game *Conflict Zone* was reviewed in terms of it aiming to revitalising RTS games by being the first RTS to attempt to 'reflect the reality of modern warfare, where campaigns involve not only military units, but civilians and media' (p 32).

> '*Conflict Zone* eschews the usual resource management found in RTS games – harvesting minerals, building bases, mining for ore or hunting for deer – and instead forces players to leverage media coverage and political ambition to win the war . . . in the cynical modern world of *Conflict Zone*, it's not enough for you to win the war, you must also woo the favour of a reluctant media . . . Set in the not too distant future, players can assume the role of a General in the ICP . . . or a rogue dictator.' (Norton-Smith, May 2001, p 32)

Some might say that this sounds similar to school leadership, but while school leaders tend to engage in strategic thinking in terms of 3- to 5-year time frames, the multimedia games environment provide problem solving scenarios for players well beyond the near future. As evidenced in the *Conflict Zone* task, children not only become the leader, they can choose their leadership style, whether they'll be a general or a rogue dictator. The new technologies can provide challenges in simulated multimedia environments which are not available in traditional text resources. However, in contrast to the often rich hi-tech, on-line home environments, children move from home to classrooms where schools struggle to fund purchases and provision of computers to enable student access. While access to computers in schools has moved a considerable distance since the disappointing finding by Jackson, Fletcher and Messer (1988) that students used a computer for only about 10 minutes each week, Oftsed (1998), in a review of information technology in UK primary schools, reported that there was limited use and unsatisfactory teaching using information technology and that 'Information technology remains the weakest subject in the primary curriculum overall'. Moreover, schools have traditionally resisted technologies which disturb the traditional ways in which teachers operate (Hodas 1993; Downes and Fatouros 1995; Cuban 1996). Culturally, schools may be compared to an immune system which attempts to resist new ideas and new technologies. Paradigms of educational thinking which aims to understand the new environments which constitute childrens' worlds is desperately needed.

The final word in defining this strategic intent of understanding children's new environments is that this requires a courageous search for truth. This involves schools being honest, both within and outside their organisations, in ways rarely evident today. We see many pictures painted of schools where 'we have lots of computers', 'our school is ahead of the rest', and 'we develop every child to their fullest potential'. A recent interview I held with a focus group of Year 8 – 12 students was a model here in the search for improved awareness and understanding. Listening to the students revealed honest perceptions and stories of their use of technologies at home and at school. They conveyed their excitement, their frustrations, the dangers, the distractions, their impatience and the ways in which positive relationships with teachers and students were enhanced by the use of the new technologies.

BOOKMARK 2: CREATING NEW ENVIRONMENTS...CLICK ON 'NEW'

'I find that a great part of the information I have was acquired by looking up something and finding something else on the way.' – Franklin P. Adams

The computer provides a non-threatening environment. Students can make mistakes and they can correct them. They are able to improve the presentation of their work which, in turn, can increase their self-esteem when their presentation is well designed. They can take pride in the quality of their published work. They can choose to share it with a range of audiences. Impatience can be alleviated by the quick and tangible results and rewards which computers can provide. Computers provide students with their need for personal space. Fear and low tolerance of failure can be reduced through allowing small steps, reinforcement and repeated tries. Hughes (in Bates, 1997), an educational psychologist, stated that 'One of the best strategies is to involve the child with EBD [emotional and behavioural difficulties] in positive and rewarding activities. Computers can help create the kind of active and motivating environment in which the learner will experience success.'

Lee (1999, p 28) indicates that school organisation still follows the Industrial Age model in which 'real learning' is seen to take place only within the walls of the school and students move in a 'lock step' movement along a 13-year production line. In proposing the way forward, Lee suggests that we need to create schools which can thrive in a networked society. Screen 2 below, adapted from the ISTE (1999) report which lists characteristics representing traditional approaches to learning and strategies associated with new learning environments, highlights the importance of facilitating learning and creating learning environments where students communicate, collaborate, and interact with others. More significantly, through the identification of these characteristics, Screen 2 provides a map for educators not only to respond to the changes occurring but to create new learning environments guided and justified by sound educational principles of effective learning and teaching.

The strategic intent of schools should be to use the new and emerging technologies to provide effective learning environments which are flexible, interactive and involve students in rich, meaningful tasks. Such environments would enable students to learn beyond the basics, beyond the traditional pedagogic benchmarks, which have tended to contribute to students becoming disengaged and unmotivated and where schooling is seen by students to be irrelevant.

Search

Screen 2: new learning environments (adapted from ISTE, 2000, p 3)

Traditional Learning Environments	*New Learning Environments*
• Teacher-centred instruction	➤ Student-centred instruction
• Single sense stimulation	➤ Multi-sensory stimulation
• Single media	➤ Multimedia
• Isolated work	➤ Collaborative work
• Information delivery	➤ Information exchange – communication
• Passive learning	➤ Active/exploratory/inquiry-based learning
• Factual, knowledge-based	➤ Critical thinking and informed decision-making
• Reactive response	➤ Proactive/planned action
• Isolated, artificial context	➤ Authentic, real-world context

New Learning Environments enable and prepare students to:

➪ *Communicate* using a wide variety of media and formats

➪ *Access and exchange information* in a variety of ways

➪ *Collaborate and cooperate* in team efforts

➪ *Interact* with others in ethical and appropriate ways

The new environments would be characterised by authentic cross-curricular approaches which have quality assured by subject experts. Quality learning resources would be developed by those subject experts in consultation with experts from other disciplines. These new environments would respond rapidly to social and technological change. Bennett and King (1997) suggest that we rarely hear the question 'What if?' and indicate that if you 'visit virtually any of America's 16,000 school districts . . . you will likely find that what's happening is what's always happened' (p 95). They argue that while we can dream and talk about the 'What if?' visions, moving them to reality takes another level of complexity and commitment. The argument developed here suggests that there is ample empirical and theoretical support for a computer education paradigm involving communication, collaboration and interaction. Nevertheless, the evidence from the national sample study of information technology skills of Australian students and teachers (Meredyth *et al*, 1999) indicates that most teachers in Australia who use computers with their students concentrate on an information model. It is likely that a similar situation exists in the USA, where only a small proportion of beginning teachers were confident of using a collaborative approach to telecommunications in 1995 (White 1997; OTA, 1995). Indeed, the OTA Report (1995, p 6) has observed that:

'The process of adopting new technologies has never been quick or effortless . . . Like all professionals, teachers have instructional methods, teaching styles, and working procedures that have served well in the past and that often reflect how they themselves were prepared. And like other large institutions, schools have organisational characteristics that make change difficult. Moreover, the unique culture of schools and changing public expectations for them create conditions substantially different from those of other workplaces.'

Increasingly, students will arrive at school with an expectation that computers and access to the Internet should be as familiar in an educational environment as they are in their own daily lives. An ongoing staff training and professional development programme is essential. Basic and advanced computing skills are insufficient. A professional learning environment needs to be nurtured where staff and students learn with the new technologies seamlessly integrated in their programmes.

BOOKMARK 3: IDENTIFYING THE IMPORTANCE OF TEACHERS . . . INSERT 'OPTIONS'

'The concept is interesting and well-formed, but in order to earn better than a "C", the idea must be feasible.' Yale University management professor in response to student Fred Smith's paper proposing reliable overnight delivery service (Smith went on to found Federal Express).

The third and critical factor in determining how successfully schools deal with the first two strategic intents of understanding and creating new learning environments is the role played by teachers and students to enable the potential to be translated into reality in schools. For example, Klein *et al* (2000) in their study of the differential effects of three types of adult interaction with kindergarten children found that adult mediating behaviours which were most predictive of children's cognitive performance were expanding, encouraging and regulation of behaviour. They concluded that integrating adult mediation in pre-school computer learning environments facilitates informed use of computer technologies and has positive effects on children's performance. Furthermore, it has now been well established that the effective integration of computers in learning environments has depended upon a change for teachers from traditional role of teacher as knowledge provider to teacher as learner and mediator of computer-assisted learning (Masters and Yelland, 1998; Salomon, 1996; Samaras, 1996). Klein *et al* (2000) concluded that children interacting with adults trained to mediate in a computer environment scored significantly higher than other children on measures of 'abstract thinking, planning, vocabulary, and visuo-motor co-ordination, and on measures of responsiveness, including measures of reflective thinking' (pp 602–603). Their study highlighted the important role of teachers as there were no differences between the performance of children who worked in a computer environment with adults available to answer their questions and others who received technical assistance only. According to Klein *et al* (2000), those findings 'support the hypothesis regarding the positive effects of working in a computer environment with an adult trained to mediate' (p 603). Screen 3, below, provides a conceptualisation of Klein *et al*'s definitions of mediation.

Search **Screen 3: Definitions and examples of mediation** (from Klein *et al*, 2000)

Definition of criteria	Examples
Focusing (intentionality and reciprocity) Any act or sequence of acts of an adult that appears to be directed toward affecting a child's perception or behaviour. These behaviours are considered reciprocal when the child responds vocally, verbally or nonverbally.	Selecting, exaggerating, accentuation, scheduling, grouping, sequencing, or pacing stimuli. Talking or handing a toy to a child is seen as intentionality and reciprocity only when it is apparent that the adult's behaviour is intentional and not accidental, and when there is an observable response from the child that he or she saw or heard the intentional behaviour.
Affecting (exciting) An adult's behaviour that expresses verbal or nonverbal excitement, appreciation, or affect, in relation to objects, animals, concepts or values.	These behaviours may include facial gestures or paralinguistic expressions (e.g. a sigh or scream of surprise), verbal expressions of affect, classification or labelling, and expressions of valuation of the child's or adult's experience.
Expanding (transcendence) An adult's behaviour directed toward the expansion of a child's cognitive awareness, beyond what is necessary to satisfy the immediate need that triggered the interaction.	Talking to a child about the qualities of food beyond what is necessary to assure provision of nutrition. Transcendence may be provided through expressions implying inductive and deductive reasoning, spontaneous comparisons, and clarification of spatial and temporal orientation.
Encouraging (mediated feelings of competence) Any verbal or nonverbal behaviour of an adult that expresses satisfaction with a child's behaviour and that identifies a specific component or components of the child's behaviour that the adult considers contributive to the experience of success.	Such identification can be achieved, for example, by careful timing of a verbal or gesture expression through reception of a desired behaviour, or through verbal and nonverbal expressions.
Regulating (mediated regulation of behaviour) Adult behaviours that model, demonstrate, and/or verbally suggest to the child regulation of behaviour in relation to the specific requirements of a task, or to any other cognitive process required prior to overt action.	Behaviour is regulated on a mediation basis by the process of matching the task requirements with the child's capacities and interests, as well as through organising and sequencing steps leading toward success. Mediated regulation may be related to the processes of perception (e.g. systematic exploration), to the process of elaboration (e.g. planning behaviour), or to the process of expressive behaviour (e.g. reducing egocentric expressions).

BOOKMARK 4: TECHNOLOGY-RELATED NEEDS . . . SELECT 'HELP'

'I have yet to see any problem, however complicated, which, when you looked at it in the right way, did not become still more complicated.' – Poul Anderson

The final strategic intent builds on the first three and, in particular, builds upon the platform of the role of teachers by suggesting the new organisation and relationships which technology enables and, indeed, demands. Screen 4 provides two contrasting images of 'kids in rows' and 'collegial classrooms'. The strategic intent enabled and demanded by the new technologies, by 'kids are different' and 'the world is different', is that of collegial, collaborative, rich learning environments. The move from 'kids in rows' to new learning environments presents challenges, difficulties and needs which have to be addressed and require support.

Search **Screen 4: from 'kids in rows' to 'collegial classrooms'**

'Kids in rows'
The room: Year 5 classroom, single teacher
The year: 2001 (but could have been 1980)
The teacher–student relationship: Teacher v. them (teacher–instructor, student–learner)
The student: Dependent upon the teacher for direction, some level of independent activity
The classroom organisation: Kids in rows
Teacher metaphor of the class: Convicts
The classroom environment: Desks in rows and separated, uninviting, little or no children's work displayed
Computers:
Little or no use, rarely turned on, covered by a sheet. Little or no access to the Internet
Behaviour management:
Reactive, controlling, based on mistrust, respect by demand, negative

'Rich, collegial classroom'
The room: A multi-age classroom, co-operative teaching partners
The year : 2001
The teacher–student relationship: Teamwork; teacher as learner, students as computer mentors
The student: Self-directed, evidence of interdependence
The classroom organisation: Individual, small group, whole class spaces, desks arranged in a variety of formations to meet different purposes
Teacher metaphor of the class: Friends
The classroom environment: Interest and learning centres, children's displays, learning extends beyond the classroom and school context, networked, connected to the world wide web, the room 'sparkles'
Computers:
Used ubiquitously, integrated into all curriculum areas and tasks, used for collaborative Internet projects
Behaviour management:
Emphasis on rich tasks, meaningful learning, student choice, trust promotes responsibility, respect is earned, positive

---

To move from 'kids in rows' to the rich learning environment of the collegial classroom isn't simple. This fourth and final strategic intent also utilises Maslow's hierarchy of needs (Norwood, 1999), namely, physiological needs, safety, belonging needs, esteem and self-actualisation needs. 'Kids in rows' at best might meet some of the practical and safety needs of the students and teachers. Clearly, though, other needs such as a sense of belonging for students are not always nurtured. Maslow believed that when those needs are not met, the person feels restless, on edge, tense, or perhaps lacking something. For example, if a child is hungry or feeling unsafe the cause is often apparent. This final strategic intent suggests strongly that the new technologies require strategies for promoting those needs to be met. Screen 5 presents a model for identifying technology-related needs to be considered by school leaders.

Search

Screen 5: technology-related needs of teachers and students

Needs	Technology Strategies
Self-Actualisation	• Creative uses of new technologies • Exploration of new technologies • Innovation and enterprise • Student and teacher control and empowerment •
Esteem	• Celebrating the acquisition of new knowledge, new skills and using new software • Displays of student work published • Participation in website and multimedia design challenges and competitions • Computer mentors, student tutors, class experts • Student and teacher knowledge and skills are capitalised upon
Belonging	• Collaborative internet projects • Team multimedia planning, design and production • Networking
Safety	• Supporting students and teachers with technophobia and cyberphobia • Administrative support • Curriculum support • Policy support
Practical	• Time to acquire technology skills • Time for training and professional development • Technical support • Access and infrastructure

SHUT DOWN OR RESTART...'RUN'

To conclude, the choice from this point for school leaders is to either shut down or restart. I urge school leaders to consider that the only difference between those two choices is the timing. To shut down will merely delay the strategic actions required to ensure that schools do not become further marginalised from the needs and worlds of students, and indeed the recognition that 'the world is different'. From here, run programs in refreshing, re-energised ways to understand and create new learning environments, identify the important and critical roles of teachers, and strategically plan to meet the technology-related needs of students and teachers.

REFERENCES

Barlow, J. P. in Tunbridge, N. (1995) The Cyberspace Cowboy. *Australian Personal Computer*. December, pp 2–4.

Bates, R. (1997) *Special Educational Needs: A Practical Guide to IT and Special Educational Needs*. Oxford: RM.

Bennett, D. A. and King, D. T. (1997) The Saturn School of Tomorrow. In King, T. (ed.). (1997). *Technology in the Classroom A Collection of Articles*. Australia: Hawker Brownlow Education. pp 95–100.

Cuban, L., (1986) *Teachers and Machines: The Classroom Use of Technology since 1920*. New York: Teachers College Press.

Downes, T. and Fatouros, C., (1995) *Learning in an Electronic World: Computers in the Classroom*. Newtown: Primary English Teaching Association.

Hodas, S., (1993) Technology Refusal and the Organisational Culture of Schools. Education Policy Analysis Archives, 1(10).

Jackson, A., Fletcher, B. and Messer, D. (1988) Effects of experience on microcomputer use in primary schools: results of a second survey. *Journal of Computer Assisted Learning*, 4, pp 214–226.

Klein, P. S., Nir-Gal, O. and Darom, E. (2000) The use of computers in kindergarten, with or without adult mediation: effects on children's cognitive performance and behavior. *Computers in Human Behavior*, (2000), 16, pp 591–608. Elsevier Science.

International Society for Technology in Education (ISTE) (2000) *National Educational Standards for Students*. Published by the International Society for Technology in Education.

Lee, M. (1998) Addressing the Teaching Inversion. *The Practising Adminis-trator*, 20, 3, pp 38–41. Fernfawn Publications, Australian Council for Educational Administration Inc.

Lee, M. (1999) A New Global Education System? *The Practising Administrator*, 21, 1, pp 28–29. Fernfawn Publications, Australian Council for Educational Administration Inc.

Lloyd, S. (1999) Hey, little spender, spend a bit more with me. *Business Review Weekly*, 27 August, 48.

Mackay, H. (1997). *Generations: Baby Boomers, their parents and their children*. Sydney: Macmillan.

Masters, J. and Yelland, N. (1996) Geometry in context: implementing a discovery-based technology curriculum with young children. Paper presented at the Australian Computers in Education Conference *Get IT*, Canberra ACT, Australia.

Meredyth, D. *et al* (October 1999) *Real Time: Computers change and schooling National Sample study of the Information Technology Skills of Australian School Students*. Australian Key Centre for Cultural and Media Policy, Canberra: Department of Education, Training and Youth Affairs (DETYA). http://www.detya.gov.au/schools/Publications/1999/realtime.pdf

Mumtaz, S. (2000) Children's enjoyment and perception of computer use in the home and the school. *Computers and Education* (May 2001), 36, 4, p 347–362. Elsevier Science.

Office of Technology Assessment, Congress of the United States (OTA) (1995) *Teachers and Technology: Making the Connection*. Washington, DC: U.S. Government Printing Office.

Norton-Smith, H. (May 2001) Conflict Zone. In *PC Powerplay*, 60, p 32–33.

Norwood, G. (1999) *Maslow's Heirarchy of Needs*. http://www.connect.net/georgen/maslow.htm

Ofsted (1998) A review of primary schools in England, (1994 – 1998). http://www.official-documents.co.uk/cgi-bin/empower

Salomon, G. (1996) Technology in a learning environment: a suggestion for a conceptual framework. In Z. Mevarech and N. Hativa, *The computer in the school*, pp 17–38. J. R. and T. A. Shoken.

Samaras, A. P. (1996) Children's computers. *Childhood Education*, 72, pp 133–136.

White, C. S., (1997) Bringing Preservice Teachers Online. In P. H. Martorella, (ed.) *Interactive Technologies and the Social Studies: Emerging Issues and Applications*, pp 27–56. Albany: State University of New York Press.

Williams, M. and McKeown, L. (1996) Definitions of the Net that teachers experience. *Australian Educational Computing*, 11 (2), 4–9.

10

Colleague support: building a supportive ecology in schools

Dr Bill Rogers

Teaching can sometimes be experienced as a lonely profession. We teach in a smallish room, with 25 to 30 students day after day after day. When the 'breaks' come we rush off for a tea or coffee, or 'playground duty' or, perhaps, another meeting. For the better part of the day we are – effectively – cut off from our adult peers, the very people whose support can make a difference to our professional and personal coping and to our professional assurance and development.

Fullan and Hargreaves (1991) have also described teaching as the 'lonely profession'. Rudduck (1991) has noted '... education is among the last vocations where it is still legitimate to work by yourself in a space that is secure against invaders.' (p 31). Is this overstated? Is there still some truth in these words in 2002? We do often work 'alone', though (hopefully) we are not lonely in our work.

There is still, in some schools, a practice of treating the class*room* as a place of professional privacy; *personal* boundedness, perhaps even professional boundedness. As Andy Miller has noted (1996), there is (in a teacher's daily role) some 'ambivalence' between the wish for 'boundedness' and the search for assistance. This ambivalence can mean that while teachers see their colleagues as a powerful source of ideas, they also see them as 'mirrors' in which they may 'assess their own performance' (pp 95–98).

This point is echoed by Leiberman and Miller (1990) when they say that,

'... loneliness and isolation are high prices to pay but teachers willingly pay them when the alternatives are seen as exposure and censure. By following the privacy rule teachers forfeit the opportunity to display their successes, but they also gain the security of not having to face their failures publicly and losing face.' (In Miller, 1996 p 94)

Hargreaves (1993) suggests,

'The culture of individualism means that most teachers are content to do their main work, classroom teaching, on their own. Sometimes this leads to isolation, loneliness, and lack of practical and moral support; but it also means being able to have one's own way without interference or hindrance from a co-professional. Not surprisingly, many teachers feel ambivalent about this professional autonomy, but will not readily choose to work with another teacher in the classroom because of its high risk of tension, disagreement or conflict.' (p 4)

Much depends, of course, on what is meant by 'enforced isolation'. It further depends on what the school encourages (or not) as colleague support, collaborative practice and professional development.

There is a creative tension regarding collegiality and collaboration when it addresses isolation as if it is a 'one-side solution' and 'collegiality as automatically good' (Fullan, 1993).

'Pushed to extremes collegiality becomes "group think"; uncritical conformity to the group, unthinking accepting of the latest solution, suppression of individual dissent.' (p 34)

Fullan and Hargreaves (1991) note that in response to the problem of isolation 'greater collegiality is becoming one of the premier improvement strategies of the 1990s'. They go on to note that in seeking to eliminate 'individualism' (habitual patterns of working alone) we should not eradicate 'individuality' (voicing of disagreement, opportunity for solitude) (p 43). Individuality (not autonomy) can generate 'creative disagreement and risk' that can be a 'source of dynamic group learning'.

The Elton Report on Discipline in Schools (1989) speaks of a tradition of 'classroom isolation' that particularly affects teachers who may be struggling in their teaching and discipline. Within such a 'tradition' teachers may believe that asking for assistance 'telegraphs' weakness, ineptness or 'incompetence'. 'Professional etiquette' may then imply that an offer of assistance from others is perceived as an implication one is ineffective. As one colleague noted to me:

'There's this ludicrous idea that when someone is really struggling we have this "hands-off mentality" – just in case we do, or say, the wrong thing. It's stupid really especially when we *know* they need help.' (cited in Rogers, 1999)

COLLEAGUE CULTURES

I have noticed that schools have varying degrees of 'consciousness' about colleague support as it is understood (and operating) in their school (Rogers, 1999 and 2001). In some schools colleague support is incidental, ad hoc,

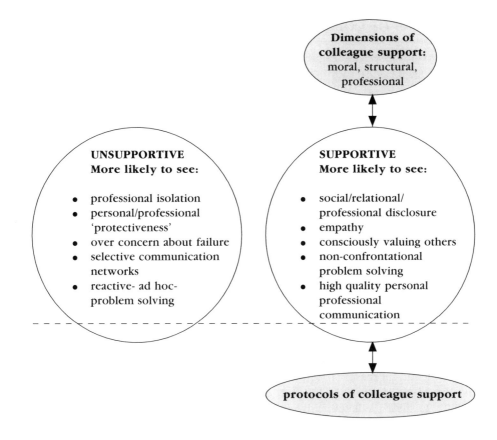

Figure 1. Contrasting cultures of support

dependent on both opportunity and trust. In schools with a 'low consciousness' of colleague support senior staff may be unaware of the need for opportunities, forms, structures, processes and procedures that specifically address the *espoused* needs of staff.

Form follows function in colleague support; the function of colleague support is the meeting of the staff needs – their fundamental needs (as a person) and their particular needs as a professional. We all have basic needs to feel valued, affirmed and to 'belong'; we all have a need to be treated as a professional and supported as a professional. 'Forms' that enable such support may be as basic as an effective 'time-out' system for one's classroom discipline and reasonable opportunities for meeting times to share common concerns through to collaborative policies that enable and support our day-to-day teaching and management.

If staff are genuinely consulted and involved in the development of these opportunities, forms, policies and plans, they feel both valued and supported.

DIMENSIONS OF COLLEAGUE SUPPORT

When I've discussed colleague support with teachers across a wide range of schools (Rogers, 1999) they commonly focus on several 'dimensions' of support.

Sharing

Sharing with colleagues, such as the sharing of ideas, resources and professional advice. Such sharing is often transitional, 'dyadic' (one-on-one), even ad hoc, but nonetheless regarded and valued for that.[1] Teachers are busy people; the assuring word and confirmation we are 'on the right track' is highly valued in a busy day. Of course such collegial sharing also operates in more formal teamings when we discuss, share, 'off-load' and plan together.

Coping under stress

Colleague support often enables staff to cope when under stress. The sharing of common concerns, needs and problems can help reframe, give assurance and reduce the stress of coping alone. There are countless studies that illustrate how colleague support buffers the normative stress of teaching, reduces emotional exhaustion and increases shared identity and problem solving. This is related to what Russell *et al* (1987, p 272) terms 'reliable alliances', where colleagues are available to give feedback, advice, encouragement and direct support. Iscoe (1974) refers to this aspect of support as describing 'the competent community' – the kind of community that fosters 'healthy connections among people' and 'catalyses and nurtures their linkages . . .' (In Hobfall, 1998, p 203).

Of course this kind of research does not simply conclude that benefits to stress reduction are directly – causatively – related to colleague support. It can be reliably inferred, however, that there is a positive relationship between 'stress buffering', 'stress reduction', 'increased coping ability' and 'social support' (from one's colleagues). See also Bernard (1990), Kyriacou (1987), Rogers (1996, 1999 and 2001). Of particular note is that measures of physical and mental health as they relate to stress management and coping are positively correlated with uncritical support from senior colleagues (supervisors). Studies by Hart *et al* (1994, 1995) illustrate that supportive leadership provides the organisational relationship that underpins all other areas of staff management; it is the 'anchor variable' that can increase or decrease staff morale.

Supportive leadership is valued when the leadership team (not just the head teacher) are 'realistically available'; where they 'enable staff to be self-reflective about professional practice as well as enabling perspective taking (of others)'. Staff feel valued when 'they are consulted on issues that count and informed on those that are routine'. Supportive leaders 'allow time for reflection on change requirements, allowing time for differences to be aired'; 'they direct support to team relationships and build team morale across the school by acknowledgment of a teacher's practice as well as affirmation, encouragement and support'; 'they make time to engage in some face-to-face communication'; 'they invite, initiate and support skills in their colleagues they may not have seen in themselves; when giving feedback they give such descriptively – with support'. Most of all, 'they invite and model respect thus inviting collegial trust'.

Few head teachers have all these qualities at all times. It is important, however, that the *leadership team* consider these aspects of supportive leadership. (From wide staff surveying on supportive leadership in Rogers, 1999 and 2001.)

Professional development

Professional support in colleague cultures enables an individual teacher's on-going professional reflection, practice and development. In supportive school cultures professional support includes on-going discussion, planning and development within the teacher's professional role and responsibilities. Professional support also needs to include feedback; both incidental encouragement and feedback on teaching and management as well as more focused professional feedback and appraisal. Our collegial peers are a significant source of knowledge, experience and skill that can be shared through informal and team-based peer discussion through to elective peer mentoring.

These 'dimensions' of colleague support are obviously inter-related and the degree to which they are *consciously* encouraged and developed by staff determines how useful, dependable and effective such support can be.

The protocols of colleague support

In the countless informal and formal discussions I have had with teachers and schools on this topic I have also noted a clear underlying aspect that teachers affirm in a supportive school culture – that of 'no-blame' support (Rogers, 1999 and 2001). In a supportive colleague ecology staff feel that they can share a range of concerns at both incidental and more formal levels without being perceived as inadequate, ineffective, or (worse) incompetent. In such schools the term 'struggling teacher' is not a simple pejorative; teachers do not believe that they have to cope alone in a kind of degrading survivalism.

Fullan and Hargreaves (1991) describe how teacher exhaustion is affected by school culture:

'One [kind of exhaustion] arises from lonely battles and unappreciated efforts, losing ground and growing and gnawing feeling of hopelessness that you cannot make a difference. The other type of exhaustion is the kind that accompanies hard work as part of a team, a growing recognition you are engaged in a struggle that is worth the effort and a recognition that what you are doing makes a critical difference for a recalcitrant child or a discouraged colleague. The former type of exhaustion ineluctably takes its toll on the motivation of the most enthusiastic teacher. The latter has its own inner reserve that allows us to bounce back after a good night's sleep. Indeed the first type of exhaustion causes anxiety and sleeplessness, while the second induces rest and regeneration of energy. School cultures make a difference in what kind of tiredness we experience.' (p 107)

I have also noted that 'consciously supportive' schools (Rogers, 1999 and 2001) are characterised by notable 'protocols' that both describe and, in a sense, delineate the 'ecology of support' present within its culture. These underlying aspects of colleague support – present in the following protocols – cross the dimensions of colleague support: moral, structural and professional. They embrace dyadic as well as the more whole-school 'structural' expressions of support – they are the enabling conditions of a consciously supportive school.

▶ **Mutual respect and mutual regard** are axiomatic to supportive collegial relations. Mutual regard refers to the regard we have (and give) for colleagues as fellow professionals and as fellow human beings. Even *basic* civility is a mark of professional respect; civility can moderate the easy selfishness that can arise when we forget what it means to be a professional and collegial community. The 'humanising' of one's professional life is well noted by Johnson (1972):

'In humanising relationships, individuals are sympathetic and responsive to human needs. They invest each other with the character of humanity, and they treat and regard each other as human. It is the positive involvement with other people that we label as humane. In a dehumanising relationship, people are divested of those qualities that are uniquely human and are turned into machines and objects. In the sense that they are treated in impersonal ways that reflect unconcern with human values.' (p 12)

Scott-Peck (1993) notes that the concept of 'personal value' is also related to 'social engagement' a 'feature of belonging essential to mental health' (p 23). This is affected, further, by the not uncommon historical aspect of classroom teaching as an isolated role experience; isolated from adult peers but ensconced with minors in classrooms.

▶ **Tolerance of (but not merely acquiescence to) fallibility in ourselves and others**: especially in areas where colleagues cope with uncertainty, normative failure and change. We won't always get it right: we forget, we 'fail', the worksheets weren't photocopied, the report wasn't in on time, the lesson didn't go the way we planned, from the bad-day-syndrome of tiredness and mistakes to Murphy's Law (or even O'Toole's Law: 'Murphy was an optimist'). Tolerance of fallibility – further – means that when we need to address (and support) others in their failure and struggle we do so with regard to their feelings and needs – within professional probity without pettiness or unreasonable criticism. I have known teachers in unsupportive school cultures who have to cope with significant stress in their teaching and discipline and exist in a kind of degrading survivalism (Rogers, 1999 and 2001). Sadly the leaders in unconsciously unsupportive schools may be unaware that their management behaviour and the way they characteristically treat struggling teachers, may be contributing to a teacher's inability to cope.

This protocol – recognising our fallibility – also works against the sort of demanding perfectionism that can create significant stress in school communities. However, where there is *characteristic* laziness, indifference, insensitivity and patterns of undermining behaviour in colleague behaviour, this will need to be supportively addressed within a school's shared values and practices. Within a whole-school perspective of shared values, aims and practices the addressing of poor or ineffective behaviour and performance in teachers is made somewhat clearer – not necessarily easier. 'Acceptance of fallibility' means acceptance of the person without denying the need, at times, to address their behaviour and support them in their struggle and failure. It is seeing a colleague's failure and struggle, not seeing *them* as a failure. In a supportive school failure is genuinely seen as a learning experience if, and when, a colleague is supported through their failure.

Humour can often play a part acknowledging and reframing our fallibility. I have noted that supportive colleague cultures exhibit shared expressions of humour: staff banter, in-house jokes, the *bon mots*, the 'court jesters', even the wry smiles that give a 'coping edge', a feeling of temporary uplift, a defusing of tension; a reframing of frustrating reality! Humour can often affirm our shared identity in a stressful profession (Burford, 1987 in Rogers, 2001).

▶ **Watchfulness and mindfulness of one another** – 'perspective taking', 'looking out for one another', 'thinking of' and 'acting for' the 'common good' of our colleagues, is a crucial protocol of colleague support. As one colleague notes, 'it is bearing one another's burdens, it is the reciprocity of good-will'. A colleague covers a class for you when you're running late; photocopies a worksheet when you're in a hurry and pigeon-holes it for you; notices your bad day and makes you a coffee; supportively notices when things are difficult and offers a 'collegial hand' and later, a chance to off-load and talk things through. Colleague 'watchfulness' can occur in the many ad hoc and transitional settings in a school day through to a conscious awareness by the leadership about what is really going on and being aware of, and sensitive to, the needs of their colleagues. In every school this aspect of 'making time for others', 'being aware of others' needs' is valued highly (Rogers, 2001). Such a 'protocol' – like that of mutual respect – carries a meaning of active effort exercised for another. It includes related meanings such as 'reliance on others' and 'dependability' and 'being sensitive to the needs of colleagues', 'looking out for one another', 'being there for others', and 'acting for the common good'. As one colleague noted, 'I know most people here would cover me if needed,' (he meant in terms of 'covering a class' – if running late – or supporting him in a crisis situation in terms of 'back-up' (Rogers, 1999).

▶ Affirming, and maintaining, a **non-competitive collegial ethos**.

▶ **Trust in both our colleagues and in supportive processes** (such as teaming, parallel planning, whole-school behaviour management policy and practice); trust in 'forms' or 'structures' of support that meet our common professional needs. Without basic trust (in our common professional role and for our common needs) it is difficult for a school to w*ork* collegially. It is important to place trust in people *and* processes; not merely in people alone.[2] Thoughtful procedures, plans and policies, while subject to human constraints and fallibility, are also vehicles for human action. Such processes can give a sense of shared purpose; of dependable organisational structure, of back-up – in short, support. Of course such processes need to be broadly and characteristically worthy of trust: time, assurance and usage will give such confirmation or otherwise. There is also *risk* with trust: I receive another; I identify with another; I extend my goodwill to another in the hope it will be accepted in good faith, honoured, even reciprocated. 'Trust has also to be exercised to be enjoyed – and that's the potential risk. But we say to the kids that they learn by "risking" – that's an acceptable "risk" ' (senior teacher; in Rogers, 1999).

There are, naturally, levels of trust in a school community, from ideas sharing and generation to having a mentor–coach relationship through to personal disclosure where private (and professional) confidences are risked. I have spoken with many colleagues who regretted even professional self-disclosure with some of their colleagues. It is not easy to rebuild trust with an individual, a team, even a whole-school staff once trust is broken and people feel 'let-down'. Without basic trust it is difficult for a school to work collegially. When staff have shared aims and structures that are dependable – such as purposeful teams, workable policies, shared planning, supportive feedback – trust is enhanced.[3] The 'risk' of trust is often rewarded. I have seen leaders who have been able to stir-up, motivate and develop skills and abilities in their team and allow and accommodate failure with encouragement and support and in doing so build up the professional growth of their staff. It is those features of trust I have noticed mostly in consciously supportive schools.

▶ **Balancing the positive and negative features** of school life and professional demands: 'keeping the bigger picture in mind', 'living with uncertainty in the long haul . . .'.

▶ **Acceptance of difference in others** (within shared values, aims and practices). A school community has a wide range of personality styles and professional expressions in teaching. There are colleagues who prefer a more 'individual' style, and those who prefer a more collegial teaching style. There are those who are more demonstrably outgoing and extrovert when sharing and teaching and those who are more reticent, less outgoing or extrovert, but no less effective as teachers. This is important when addressing the issue of differences in ideas, approaches, opinions and teaching/management style and practice.

Colleagues frequently noted that in more collegially supportive schools their differences were accepted; even acknowledged (Rogers, 1999). Differences of opinion and practice, even healthy conflict, are part of a school's social and organisational fabric. People in a team should be able to argue without destroying the team. This, in fact, may be a strength of the team when:

> 'New norms that directly pertain to complex and difficult problems include: bringing uncomfortable issues out into the open (and) persist in drawing attention to problems even if others seem reluctant to consider the implications of what you are saying; listen to other members' viewpoints even if you disagree with them; encourage zany and bizarre perspectives to ensure that nothing important and possible has been overlooked; make people aware when a topic that should generate a heated debate has not.' (Kilmann, 1985, p 66)

A healthy organisation responds neither passively nor rebelliously to demands from outside itself. Because it equates growth with a collaborative style it is likely to measure goals from a flexible stance, but with a keen eye for that which is good from the past; not mere change for change's sake as a new form of pedantry. Collaboration is a means of adaptation; it has *in place* problem-solving mechanisms enabling it critically to face new pressures and demands.

▶ **Shared professional assurance**: at the dyadic and transitional (ad hoc) level, as well as the more involved team level. The need for assurance that one is meeting one's professional obligations is an important professional need.

▶ **Being purpose-driven rather than merely task-driven**. This feature of colleague support is strongest when aspects of teaming and teams is functional, purposeful and on-going. A notable feature of supportive collegiality occurs when the team's existence has meaning not just for meeting their professional obligations and the needs of the individuals in the team but for the school's purpose and mission. A key feature – perhaps the main feature – of school-wide consciousness of support is highlighted in the observable, conscious difference between mutual obligation as a 'personal construct' and mutual obligation as a characteristic 'school-wide expression' of school values and practice. As one of my colleagues notes, in contrasting her past school with her current school: 'The difference here is, **I could rely on anyone not just a particular colleague at a particular time**; or if the mood was OK . . .' (colleague's emphasis; cited in Rogers, 1999).

▶ **The 'certainty of uncertainty'**; this seemingly paradoxical protocol reminds us that things do not always go to plan – certainly in day-to-day teaching. This does not negate the obvious and essential need to plan, structure, develop policy and seek to manage our part of the world as teachers with some reasonable consistency. It does reduce the unrealistic and stressful striving for perfection. As one wag once wrote 'for every complex problem there is a simple solution and that solution is wrong.'

▶ **Commitment to face-to-face communication**. This feature of collegiality is evidenced in dyadic and team contexts. What staff value is the moral support that face-to-face communication gives from the transitional 'whinge' (coping support and moral support) through to the effective practice of collaborative communication in teams (Rogers, 1999).

DEVELOPING A SUPPORTIVE COLLEAGUE CULTURE

In consciously supportive schools the 'consciousness of colleague support' moves from a 'personal construct' to a 'social construct' in key areas such as:

▶ **purposeful teaming** with an emphasis on professional planning and coping strategies, as well as aspects of social coping such as managing stress by directly talking things though with one's colleagues in the team. Such professional sharing provides relief not just of normative stress but it also works for shared, 'owned' solutions in the longer term.

▶ **a consistent, school-wide policy framework and practice**, particularly in the naturally stressful area of behaviour management and discipline.

▶ **back-up support in discipline situations,** notably in the use of short-term 'time-out' practices and conflict resolution processes with difficult students, classes and even parents! Such back-up is essential in enabling and supporting teachers (and students) in crisis management and follow-up.

▶ **professional feedback** and professional development as teachers consciously take time to reflect on their teaching, pedagogy, management and discipline.

Colleague support, of course, cannot be mandated: '. . . we cannot mandate what matters to effective practice . . . the more complex the change the less you can force it' Fullan, 1993, (p 21). The anomaly regarding colleague support is that a central feature of our professional life and personal coping cannot simply be forced from (or on) our colleagues; it is more likely to characteristically occur when staff value, endorse, encourage and model collegiality and support within an ecology of mutual regard rather than mandating such support. This is particularly important for school leadership a concept explored by Fullan (1987, 1993), Hargreaves (1993). Fullan and Hargreaves (1991) point out that 'many staff initiatives take the form of something that is done to teachers rather than with them, still less by them' (p 17).

Form *follows* function; the function of colleague support is to meet colleague needs. One of the ways to determine colleagues' needs is to undertake a periodic school-wide review (informally and formally). There is a difference between perceived needs and espoused needs. Where a school leadership takes colleagues' needs seriously (based on such a review) staff feel valued, supported and motivated to engage with change.

This is a point acknowledged in the Elton Report on School Discipline (1989):

'The way in which a school is run can be changed. We know this is not easy. Changing the nature of an institution can be a long, complicated and uncomfortable process. We recognise that the difficulties involved in breaking into the vicious circle of ineffective performance and low morale can be very great, and that some schools may need a great deal of help in achieving this breakthrough. We are convinced however from what we have seen in schools, from research evidence, and from experiences described to us in other countries that successful change can be achieved. The first or important requirement is a positive commitment to change by the head teacher and other senior staff. The second is for them to carry as many of the rest of the staff as possible with them and to be open to their suggestions.' (p 90)

Schools are at differing levels of school-wide 'consciousness' about colleague support; its provision, its normative expression, its 'utility' (Rogers, 2001). If a school is to move beyond dyadic and 'transitional' expressions of support it will need to provide regular (and dependable) forms, options, structures, processes and policies that enhance and enable colleague support, particularly in the area of behaviour management and discipline.

Those 'more consciously supportive' schools will often be evaluating their current expressions of, and provision of, colleague support. Some schools may only need to fine-tune or adapt current structures or policies. Other schools will need to engage in substantial change. Those schools that are less consciously supportive will need a more extensive needs-analysis, as their structure and forms of support may be limited, unhelpful or not focused on (or meeting) colleague needs. In such schools awareness-raising about the benefits of focused colleague support as well as addressing appropriate forms and structures will also be helpful (Rogers, 2001).

Needs analysis and evaluating current position

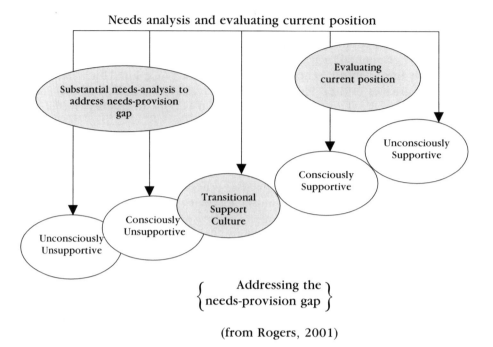

{ Addressing the }
{ needs-provision gap }

(from Rogers, 2001)

Figure 2. Needs analysis 'continuum' and consciousness of support

In pursuing adaptive facility, from the 'typology of consciousness of support' (see Figure 2) schools will enter into some kind of school-wide review that will need to address issues such as:

► Where is the school now in terms of its 'consciousness' of colleague support?
► How *acknowledged* are the individual and collective needs of colleagues?
► What changes need to be made to address, and seek to meet, staff colleague support needs?
► What changes to current forms, structures, processes or plans will we need to make?

While the review process will vary in degree, the fundamental process will:

► Acknowledge the need for colleague support beyond natural, transitional, expressions of support.
► Identify needs (espoused needs) and evaluate needs-provision among staff.
► Appraise the needs-provision gap (some needs will be more generic, some more specific).
► Decide on the focus for any changes and possible areas for change (always

explaining any changes and providing support for the change process), emphasising mutual responsiveness and mutual regard for 'our common lot'.

▶ Develop action options and plans to enhance and motivate task engagement and management.

▶ Commit to an on-going review process.

CONCLUSION

The English novelist George Eliot said 'What do we live for if it is not to make life less difficult for each other?' At the heart of colleague support is that shared humanity, without which any meaningful common activity is much more difficult. The days are long gone when teachers had to work in professional isolation, anxious perhaps that others might negatively assess and rate them. Collaboration and collegiality are not simplistic notions or some easy formula for 'successful support'; rather they are the necessary condition for likely, constructive and purposeful support in our profession. When colleagues believe and feel they are valued, both their basic human needs as well as their professional needs are more likely to be met. When a school leadership *consciously* values, affirms, models and develops supportive options, structures, policies, teaming and behaviour, then there is a basis for an ecology of support. When the 'protocols', noted earlier, are normatively present (even on our 'bad days') teaching will not be as stressful as often, as long – indeed, within such an ecology of support our teaching will have that professional collegiality necessary for professional assurance and professional esteem.

ENDNOTES

Note: Some of the material in this article is drawn from an article in *Educare*: Colleague Support: Making a difference (2000); some is drawn from Rogers, 1999 (unpublished doctoral dissertation) and some from a work in print (Rogers, 2001), *I get by with a little help* . . .

1 As Middlebrook (1974) notes 'The two-person group (dyad): it is important to note (that) a great deal of social interaction takes place on a one-to-one basis (pp 412–416).

2 A point well made by Hargeaves (1994): 'Trust can be invested in persons or in processes – in the qualities and conduct of individuals, or in the expertise and performance of abstract systems. It can be an outcome of meaningful face-to-face relationships or a condition of their existence' (p 39).

3 As Shaw (1987) develops this concept he notes that: 'trust-based relation-ships presuppose a broad measure of shared goals within the institution, so that there is ample scope for social rather than economically calculated exchanges. From the point of view of school management, "goodwill"

which assumes a readiness to undertake unspecified obligations is much preferable to contract, where attempts are made to impose particular obligations – low trust is made more explicit, non-reciprocal exchanges are demanded, and a power conflict atmosphere draws a step nearer.' (p 783).

4   Saul (1990) gives a salient reminder here: 'The virtue of uncertainty is not a comfortable idea, but then a citizen-based democracy is built on participation, which is the very expression of permanent discomfort. The corporatist system depends on the citizen's desire for inner comfort. Equilibrium is dependent upon our recognition of reality, which is the acceptance of permanent psychic discomfort. And the acceptance of psychic discomfort is the acceptance of consciousness.' (1996, p 195).

REFERENCES

Axworthy, D., Olney, H. and Hamilton, P. (1989) Managing Student Behaviour: A Whole School Approach. In *Addressing Behaviour Problems in Australian Schools*. Camberwell, Vic.: ACER.

Bernard, M. (1990) *Taking the Stress Out of Teaching*. Melbourne: Collins.

Elton Report (1989) *Discipline in Schools, Report of the Committee of Inquiry*. London: Her Majesty's Stationery Office.

Frankyl, V. (1963) *Man's Search for Meaning* (An Introduction to Logotherapy). New York: Simon and Schuster.

Fullan, M. (1993) *Change Forces: Probing the Depths of Educational Reform*. London: Falmer Press.

Fullan, M. and Hargreaves, A. (1991) *What's Worth Fighting For?: Working Together For Your School*. Toronto: Ontario Public School Teachers' Federation.

Hargreaves, A. (1991) Continued collegiality: a micropolitical analysis'. In Blase, J. (ed.) *The Policies of Life in Schools*. New York: Sage.

Hart, P. M. (1994) Teacher Quality of Life: Integrating work experiences, psychology distress and morale. *Journal of Occupational and Organisational Psychology* 67, pp 109–139.

Hart, P. M., Wearing, A. J. and Conn, M. (1995) Wisdom is a poor predictor of the relationship between discipline policy, student misbehaviour and teacher stress. *British Journal of Educational Psychology* 1195, 65, pp 27–48.

Hobfoll, S. E. (1998) Stress, Culture and Community: *The Psychology and Philosophy of Stress*. New York: Plenum Press.

Johnson, D. W. (1972) *Reaching Out: Interpersonal Effectiveness and Self-Actualization*. Needham Heights, MA: Simon and Schuster.

Kilmann, R. (1985) Organisations and change. *Psychology Today*, April, 1987 pp 65–67.

Kyriacou, C. (1981) Social support and occupational stress among school teachers. *Educational Studies* 7, pp 55–60.

Kyriacou, C. (1987) Teacher appraisal in the classroom: Can it be done? *School*

Organisation. 7, 2, pp 139–144.

Kyriacou, C. (1987) Teacher Stress and Burnout: An International Review. *Educational Research* 29, 2, pp 145–152.

Lieberman, A. (ed.) (1990) *School as Collaborative Cultures: Creating the Future Now.* Basingstoke: Falmer Press.

Middlebrook, P. (1974) *Social Psychology and Modern Life.* New York: A.A. Knopf.

Miller, A. (1996) *Pupil Behaviour and Teacher Culture.* London: Cassell.

Rogers, B. (1996) *Managing Teachers' Stress.* London: Pitman.

Rogers, B. (2001) *I get by with a little help . . . Colleague support in schools.* Melbourne: Australian Council for Educational Research.

Rudduck, J. (1991) *Innovation and Change.* Milton Keynes: Open University.

Russell, D. W., Altimaier, E. and Van Velzen, D. (1987) Job Related Stress, Social Support and Burnout Among Classroom Teachers. *Journal of Applied Psychology* 72, 2, pp 269–274.

Saul, R. (1990) *The Unconscious Civilisation.* Ringwood, Victoria: Penguin Books.

Scott-Peck, M. (1993) *A World Waiting To Be Born: Civility Rediscovered.* New York: Bantam Books.

Shaw, K. E. (1987) Skills, control and the mass professions. *The Sociological Review* 25, 4, 775–794.

Shulman, L. S. (1988) A Union of Insufficiencies: Strategies for Teacher Assessment in a Period of Reform. *Educational Leadership* 46 (3), pp 36–41.

Conclusion

Professional reflection is crucial to professional growth. As we reflect on our teaching experience and practice we learn. If that learning is to be purposeful such reflection has to be conscious, on-going and set within a supportive collegial community.

When we're under the daily pressures of teaching, when we have to 'deliver the goods' day after day, it is easy – naturally easy – to get so caught up in the daily demands of teaching that professional reflection is sidelined. It isn't that we do not value such reflection it is rather that making time for such *purposeful* reflection is difficult; more so, perhaps, with the issue of discipline and behaviour management. Though such reflection is essential to effective teaching and positive, co-operative classroom environments, teachers can go a long time before they re-assess what they do and why. Conscious reflection on what we do in our daily discipline and management is essential to our professionalism and to our sense of purpose in this area.

I once had an older colleague say to me 'You can't teach an old dog new tricks.' We were in a small collegial peer-group discussing behaviour and discipline issues in our classes. The aim of the group was to reflect on what we *characteristically* did – and to discuss why; we discussed what we were aiming for and what differences we believed such discipline and behaviour management made in our classes. I replied, 'But you're not a dog – you're a human being' (and I meant it). I got the wry smile in return and we went on to discuss the differences between 'tricks', 'age', 'experience', 'utility', 'compliance', 'co-operation' and much more. It was a conscious, reflective session with good humour, eventual goodwill and commitment to professional change.

In the end teachers do what they do based on a mix of 'pragmatism', 'utility', 'expectation', 'policy imperative' and – hopefully – principle. The behaviour management and discipline issues, concerns, trends, practice and skills – shared in these essays – are humane, realistic, conscious of practical utility and purposeful. The aim is always to enable students to 'own' their behaviour in a way that respects the rights of others. The aim of my colleagues – constantly emphasised in these essays – is that 'good' discipline and management and teaching are not separate issues or concerns. They also consistently affirm and encourage us to remember that the building and sustaining of positive relationships is a crucial feature of any aspect of teacher (or school) discipline. That creative tension between personal and social responsibility is present in each writer's emphasis and approach. In their more reflective moments teachers are – hopefully – conscious not only of what they do but why they do what they do as professionals. As Shulman (1988) notes:

'Teachers will become better educators when they can begin to have explicit answers to the questions, 'How do I know what I know? How do I know the reasons for what I do? Why do I ask my students to perform or think in particular ways?' The capacity to answer such questions not only lies at the heart of what we mean by becoming skilled as a teacher; it also requires a combining of reflection on practical experience and reflection on theoretical understanding.' (p 33)

There is much in these essays that repays such reflection and supports purposeful change. I trust these essays will both inform and encourage such reflection and change in your own teaching and leadership journey.

Index